Foreword

Merchants by tradition use shorthand expressions to describe their respective obligations connected with the carriage of goods under international contracts of sale. This practice – important and rational as it may be – involves serious risks of misunderstanding. Ever since 1936, the International Chamber of Commerce (ICC) has provided rules of interpretation for the most important trade terms used by merchants in international trade, thereby greatly contributing to trade facilitation. Indeed, trade terms constitute the most important element of the international contract of sale, since they purport to tell the contracting parties what to do, and thereby provide an indispensable tool for the implementation of their contract.

Incoterms themselves do not have the same status as provisions of national sale of goods acts or of international conventions, such as the 1980 International Convention on International Sale of Goods. Indeed, the Convention does not deal at all with trade terms, since this matter was left to the ICC. The ICC is better suited than the legislator to ensure through ICC National Committees worldwide that the rules of interpretation correspond to current practices with respect to transport handling techniques, documentation and export and import formalities. One example are the provisions of the A8-clauses of Incoterms 1990, where electronic data interchange (EDI) has been given particular attention.

Although Incoterms, which merely constitute rules of interpretation, do not have the same status as legal provisions, they may – at least in some areas of the world – be accepted as international custom of the trade, and thereby gain the same effect as agreed contract terms (cf. art. 9 of the Convention). This is true even though the contracting parties are well advised to make express reference to Incoterms in connection with their choice of the appropriate term so as to avoid any dispute with respect to their legal effect.

Because Incoterms have been officially recognised by the ICC as authoritative rules of interpretation, their wording – particularly because of the need to make them applicable worldwide – is of necessity somewhat general and abstract. In this sense, they resemble legal provisions as drafted in national sale of goods acts and the Convention. This has necessitated the creation of a Guide in order to make Incoterms easier to read and understand by merchants. It should be stressed that the Guide does not have the same status as Incoterms themselves and that, as the author of the Guide, I have to bear the responsibility for any of its shortcomings. In a sense, though, it can be said that the Guide more or less serves in the same manner as do explanatory notes or *travaux préparatoires* to legal provisions.

The present book, *Incoterms in Practice,* has yet another use. It has been written by experts with a profound knowledge of trade practices, and thus contains practical advice to the merchant with respect to the various applications of Incoterms in different circumstances regarding contract of carriage, documents, EDI, documentary credits (UCP 500), insurance and the passing of national borders inside or outside of regional markets, such as the European Union. The particular problems connected with the FCA term – the modern FOB – are addressed here, as well as the difficult problem of the relation between the contract of sale and the contract of carriage. There is also discussion of the need for further specificity by the authors' offering variants of, and additions to, Incoterms themselves. Finally, the questions on Incoterms, which have been answered by the Panel of Experts set up as an additional service to the users of Incoterms, are the subject of a separate, highly useful, chapter.

In my position as Chairman of the Incoterms Working Party, where all the contributors to this book regularly meet and generously offer their time and expertise, I am convinced that their presentations in this book will greatly enhance the future use and understanding of Incoterms.

JAN RAMBERG
Chairman of the ICC Working Party on Incoterms

Preface

This book presents to users of *Incoterms 1990* a series of essays focusing on specific aspects of Incoterms. The book falls broadly into two parts. The first five chapters look at the relationship between Incoterms and the various contracts involved in international trade, for example the contract of carriage and the letter of credit. The second five chapters concentrate on specific issues relating to the application and interpretation of Incoterms, for example questions raised by the European Single Market and problems arising from terminal handling charges.

The book was conceived in 1993 as a result of the interest shown by international traders and members of the International Chamber of Commerce in various practical issues associated with the use of Incoterms. The selection of writers and of the ground to be covered was co-ordinated by Guillermo Jimenez, Head of Division at the ICC, with the assistance of Jean Guédon, member of the French National Committee of the ICC. As a result of their efforts, we have a panel of writers drawing on a broad wealth of practical experience.

The writers' views and comments on Incoterms are based on their own personal experience of the workings of Incoterms in practice. In this sense, the book is more of a comment than a guide, and therefore takes nothing away from the primacy of the official ICC publications, *Incoterms 1990* and the *Guide to Incoterms 1990*. Unlike those publications, this book, though produced by ICC Publishing SA, bears no official *imprimatur* of the ICC. Indeed, as a collection of individual observations of Incoterms in practice by toilers in the field, this book could hardly have come at a better time, coming as it does half-way through the usual time-span of the current version of Incoterms.

I was recruited as General Editor and writer of the first chapter late in 1994 after the majority of the manuscripts had been submitted to the ICC. Consequently, many thanks are due, some retrospective to my own involvement and all owed in a more than purely customary fashion. First, I must thank the writers for having patiently borne the burden of editorial review, exercised – I hope – gently and with restraint. Here at Southampton, I must recognise the valuable help given to me by Emily Camilleri and Raffaella Bonadies, two LL.M. students who gave research assistance at different stages of the project. Finally in Paris, the work would not have seen the light without the efforts of Pascale Reins, who cheerfully and charmingly encouraged us all towards timely and contractual delivery. To these and to many others, my sincere thanks.

To the readers, I hope you will find in the following chapters much that is challenging, instructive and useful.

CHARLES DEBATTISTA
Southampton
April 1995

Contents

Incoterms and the Contract of Carriage

CHARLES DEBATTISTA

Introduction

Whenever goods are sold across international boundaries, the seller and the buyer will be concerned with the carriage of the goods sold and with the contract governing such carriage. The contract of carriage is therefore necessarily relevant, albeit to varying degrees, to all the terms of sale contained in Incoterms 1990: each incoterm will allocate the costs and risks of carriage to one or other of the parties to the contract of sale.

However, to examine in practical detail the points of contact between each incoterm and the relevant contract of carriage would take more space than this book allows. This chapter will therefore concentrate on the "C"-terms, and more particularly on the paradigm "C"-term, the CIF incoterm, focusing on the obligations imposed by this term of the contract of sale regarding the contract of carriage which the seller must conclude with the carrier and pass to the buyer.

The central thrust of the chapter will be a well-known proposition always worth repeating, namely that costly disputes between exporters and importers frequently arise where contracts are drafted with little regard to the terms of other contracts involved in the same transaction. A failure to match the contracts of sale, carriage, insurance and the letter of credit commonly lies at the bottom of misunderstandings which lead at best to delay and at worst to litigation.

The purpose of this chapter will be to identify the duties of the seller under the CIF incoterm regarding the contract of carriage which the seller is to conclude under the contract of sale.

The various carriage duties are imposed in particular by articles A3(a), A4, A6, A7 and A8. These carriage obligations can be grouped under four heads, relating respectively to the terms of the contract of carriage, the shipment of the goods, the route of shipment and the discharge of the goods. The central questions throughout will be: what does the CIF incoterm tell us about the type of carriage contract which the seller must procure for the buyer; what practical problems might arise as between seller and buyer; and how might these problems be avoided or solved?

An important preliminary point needs to be made. The comments made in this chapter are based on English law. Incoterms do not exist in a vacuum: although they provide a skeleton of terms, these terms can only survive within the body of a contract of sale. Moreover, for the contract to live it needs the oxygen of a governing law and the governing law will be assumed in this chapter to be English law. It is hoped, however, that the chapter will nonetheless provide a list of practical issues which might also be relevant to lawyers advising exporters and importers incorporating Incoterms 1990 into contracts of sale governed by other legal systems.

I The terms of the contract of carriage

Article A3(a) of the CIF incoterm imposes on the seller the duty to "[c]ontract on usual terms ... for the carriage of the goods." The word "usual" again surfaces in article A8, which imposes on the seller the duty to provide the buyer with the "usual transport document." What does this word "usual" mean? Money turns on the point because if the buyer can successfully argue that the contract of carriage procured by the seller is "unusual", then the seller is in breach and is liable in damages for any loss which this breach might have caused. Moreover, if the contract of carriage concluded by the seller is not "reasonable having regard to the nature of the goods and the other circumstances of the case" then the buyer may choose to refuse to treat delivery to the carrier as delivery under the contract of sale[1]. This option may be extremely useful to a buyer who has, for purely commercial reasons, lost interest in the goods. The content of the seller's duty to provide the buyer with a "usual" or "reasonable" contract of carriage is therefore of considerable significance and a number of points need to be made.

1 Express terms about the carriage contract in the sale contract

The first and most obvious point – frequently ignored – is that if the buyer is particularly anxious that the contract of carriage procured by the seller should contain or exclude a particular term, then the best way to ensure this is to stipulate appropriately and expressly in the contract of sale.

Thus, for example, if refrigeration of the goods at a particular temperature is crucial to the buyer, the best guarantee that the goods will be carried at that temperature – and more importantly, that there will be effective remedies against the carrier if they are not – is for the contract of sale expressly to stipulate that the seller will procure a contract of carriage stipulating for such refrigeration. If the contract of sale contains an express stipulation requiring the seller to procure a contract of carriage imposing a duty on the carrier to maintain the goods at a particular temperature, the test of the seller's performance under the contract of sale is no longer whether the contract of carriage is "usual" under Incoterms. The question now becomes: does the contract of carriage procured by the seller comply with the requirements made of that contract by the contract of sale?

The drafting of appropriate terms in the contract of sale will concentrate the seller's mind when negotiating the terms of the contract of sale.

2   "Usual" choice of law and forum clauses?

Does the seller's duty to procure a "usual" contract of carriage give the buyer a right to insist on a contract of carriage governed by any particular legal system with disputes to be resolved in any particular forum? The answer to this question in extreme situations is tolerably clear. Thus, were the seller to procure a contract of carriage providing for arbitration in a war zone, it is suggested that this would put the seller in breach of his contract of sale. At the other extreme, a seller is definitely not in breach if he procures a contract of carriage covered by the Hague, Hague-Visby or Hamburg Rules. However unreasonable some might think certain terms of these Rules might be, the regimes established by these Conventions are definitely "usual". More difficult situations may occur: thus, for example, what if the seller procures a contract of carriage which is governed by a system of law which picks none of these three "usual" regimes, but chooses one which unreasonably excludes the carrier's liability for loss? Would this be a "usual" contract of carriage?

It is suggested that a court would tread very cautiously along a path which put the seller in breach of his contract of sale in such circumstances. Again, however, doubt and possible litigation could be avoided through appropriate drafting in the contract of sale. If the buyer wishes to ensure tender by the seller of a bill of lading incorporating one of the three "usual" carriage regimes, a clause to that effect could easily and effectively be drafted into the contract of sale.

3 Bill of lading containing a reference to a charterparty

Article A8 of the CIF incoterm imposes on the seller the duty to provide the buyer with a copy of the charterparty "if the transport document contains a reference to a charterparty." Two separate issues arise.

First, the precise circumstances in which this duty applies are not at all clear. Bills of lading referring to charterparties come in two broad forms. In certain trades, particularly in commodities, bills of lading are frequently drafted and issued for use in close conjunction with named charterparties[2]. However, in general trade where goods happen to be carried on a chartered vessel, it is not uncommon to find references to a charterparty, in whole or in part, in standard form bills of lading. Such bills are intended for use quite independent from charterparties and yet do contain a reference to a charterparty. Now it is beyond doubt that the CIF incoterm imposes a duty on the seller to tender a copy of the charterparty in the first case. However, is this also the case where the bill of lading is a stand-alone bill which happens to seek to incorporate a term or terms from a charterparty[3]? From the buyer's point of view, the danger with such a bill of lading is that his rights and liabilities vis-a-vis the carrier are contained in a document which he has not seen, much less negotiated: the least he would wish for is notice of such rights and liabilities through tender of the charterparty under the contract of sale.

Given the doubts about the precise ambit of this part of article A8 of the CIF incoterm, a buyer concerned to avoid the risk would be well-advised to draft an express term into his contract of sale imposing on the seller a duty to tender the charterparty with any bill of lading which contains **any** reference to a charterparty, however slight[4].

Secondly, it is clear that if, under the law of carriage of goods by sea, terms are effectively incorporated from the charterparty into the bill of lading, then the terms thus incorporated form an integral part of the contract of carriage tendered by the seller to the buyer and must therefore themselves be "usual" and must conform to any relevant stipulations in the contract of sale. Thus, for example, if the contract of sale provides for discharge in a particular manner at a particular port, but a charterparty clause incorporated into the bill of lading allows for discharge in another manner unavailable at the discharge port, then it is suggested that the seller would be in breach of his duty under the contract of sale to procure and tender a contract of carriage which complies with his obligations under the contract of sale.

4 Continuous documentary cover and Incoterms

For the seller to perform his duty to tender a "usual" contract of carriage, the contract tendered must provide the buyer with **continuous documentary cover** against the carrier. This means two things: first, the seller must provide the buyer with a document which gives the buyer a contract enforceable by him against the carrier. The document tendered must give the buyer legal *locus standi* against the carrier[5]. Secondly, the cover afforded to the buyer by the contract of carriage must contain no gaps. Thus, for example, where a seller tendered a bill of lading covering only the second leg of a voyage during which goods were transhipped, the seller was held to be in breach of his obligations under a c.i.f. contract[6].

The duty to provide the buyer with continuous documentary cover may cause difficulties where the goods are carried in containers, difficulties which illustrate the importance of choosing the right incoterm for the mode of transport envisaged.

Where a sale contract expressed to be on c.i.f. terms incorporates Incoterms 1990 and the goods are delivered to the carrier at an inland depot in a container, is the seller in breach of his sale contract if he tenders a bill of lading imposing responsibility on the carrier only from port to port? On the one hand, the seller would appear to have performed his duties under A3 and A8. He will have contracted "on usual terms ... for the carriage of the goods to the named port of destination by the usual route in a seagoing vessel" (A3) – usual, at any rate, for a sale contract expressed to be on c.i.f. terms. Likewise, he will be able to provide "the usual transport document" under article A8, again "usual" at any rate for a contract expressed to be on c.i.f. terms. On the other hand, the seller is arguably in breach of article A4 which imposes on the seller the duty to "deliver the goods on board the vessel at the port of shipment," the seller having in fact delivered the goods at an inland depot. Money turns on the issue because the buyer[7] may find himself unable to recover against the carrier if the goods are damaged between the inland point and the discharge port. The problems here are caused by the all too common error of using the CIF incoterm where the CIP incoterm would have been more appropriate.

II Shipment of the goods

The CIF incoterm imposes several obligations on the seller regarding the shipment of the goods. These duties cover five main areas: notification of shipment; quantity of goods shipped; shipment on board; the date of shipment; and the payment of the freight. We shall deal with each of these in turn.

1 Notification of shipment

Article A7 imposes on the seller the duty to "[g]ive the buyer sufficient notice that the goods have been delivered on board the vessel." This notification is known to international trade practitioners as the "notice of appropriation" or the "declaration of shipment". Its purpose is to enable the buyer to make discharge arrangements or to enable him to sell the goods on by describing them as the goods on the named ship. In English law the notice has an impact on the seller's duties regarding both the goods and the documents. Once the notice has been sent, the seller can only perform his physical duties by shipping goods on the named ship or procuring goods on it. Moreover, the seller can only perform his documentary duties by tendering documents covering goods on the named vessel.

The contract of sale will typically contain detailed terms about establishing the contents, form and time in which the notice must be sent to the buyer[8]. Problems arise where the seller sends a formally valid but substantively inaccurate notice. The seller may, for example, send a notice of appropriation complying in all respects with the requirements of the contract of sale as to contents, form and time, but failing accurately to give the name of the ship actually used. In this situation, the seller is at considerable risk. If the buyer loses interest in the goods, or at any rate loses interest in paying the contract price, he may be able either to reject the transport document on tender or to accept the documents without prejudice and recover the difference between the contract price and the current, lower, market price[9]. There are two ways in which the seller can avoid this type of risk. The first and the more obvious is to ensure that the notice of appropriation he sends to the buyer is accurate. The second is to draft a term into the sale contract allowing him to substitute the notice of appropriation[10].

It is clear that matters as to the form of the notice of appropriation and as to its possible substitution by the seller are matters not covered by article A7 of the CIF incoterm and that parties' concerns in this area can only be catered for through appropriately drafted clauses in the contract of sale.

2   The contract goods

The goods shipped must be the contract goods and the documents tendered must be documents covering the contract goods: article A4 states that the seller must "[d]eliver the goods on board the vessel" and article A8 rather more explicitly states that the document tendered by the seller must "cover the contract goods."

Three points need to be made here. First, the documents tendered must be for the contract quantity, for no less and for no more[11].

Secondly, the documents tendered must be for the entire contract quantity: the seller has no right or duty to tender to the buyer bills of lading covering parts of the cargo unless this is specifically provided for in the contract of sale[12]. Thirdly, a transport document giving the quantity of the goods but qualifying them with the words "weight and quantity unknown" or words to that effect is a document for the contract goods despite the qualification[13].

3   Shipped on board

Article A4 imposes on the seller the duty to deliver the goods "on board the vessel at the port of shipment." Two points need to be made here. In the nature of things, this duty needs to be interpreted in a somewhat relaxed manner where the seller is not the shipper but an intermediate seller in a string. Presumably such a seller in a sale contract incorporating Incoterms 1990 would equally well perform his obligations by tendering documents stating that the goods had been shipped, albeit prior to the moment when the contract of sale was concluded.

Secondly, article A4 makes it clear that where the sale is expressed to be on c.i.f. terms and Incoterms 1990 are incorporated, the seller must tender a document stating that the goods have actually been shipped on board: tender of a bill of lading stating that the goods have been received for shipment would constitute a breach of the contract of sale[14]. This requirement will cause difficulty where goods are sold in containers on c.i.f. terms. The bill of lading issued by the carrier may here very well state simply that the goods have been received for shipment and the buyer may well be in a position to reject the document for breach of article A4. To avoid this risk, where goods are carried in containers, the appropriate incoterm to use is the CIP term, which provides at article A4 for delivery "into the custody of the carrier".

4   Date of shipment

Article A4 imposes on the seller the duty to ship the goods "on the date or within the period stipulated" in the contract of sale. This duty is translated into a documentary duty in article A8 which states that the transport document "must be dated within the period agreed for shipment". Thus where the sale contract provides for "September shipment", the goods must be shipped in September and the bill of lading must be dated in September.

Under English law, the date of shipment is treated as part of the description of the goods, a condition of the contract of sale under section 13 of the Sale of Goods Act 1979, breach of which entitles the buyer to reject the documents on tender and/or sue for damages[15]. This is why it is quite common to come across bills of lading which state that the goods were shipped on the last date of the stipulated month: rather than expose himself to action by the buyer for breach of the contract of sale, the seller may persuade the carrier to issue a bill of lading dated within the shipment period despite the fact that shipment has actually been completed outside that period. While this practice has the attraction of oiling the wheels of the transaction, it is not without problems.

The first is that the carrier is only likely to agree to the seller's request if the seller issues a letter of indemnity holding the carrier harmless against any consequences of having mis-dated the bill of lading. Such a letter of indemnity may well be unenforceable by the carrier against the shipper, based as it is on fraud[16]. Moreover, even if the letter of indemnity were enforceable, there are still costs incurred in issuing it, given that carriers will frequently insist on its being backed by a first class bank.

The second problem for the seller is his liability to the buyer if he is found out. By tendering a bill of lading which complied on its face with the shipment period in the contract of sale but which did not tell the truth, the seller deprives the buyer of the opportunity of rejecting the document on tender, an opportunity worth much to the buyer where the market price drops below the contract price at the time the documents are tendered. If the buyer discovers that he has been deceived into payment in this way, he can sue the seller for the difference between the contract price and the market price at the time the buyer discovers that the document had been mis-dated[17].

5   Payment of freight

Articles A3 and A6 make it clear that the freight must be paid by the seller. A3 imposes upon the seller the duty to contract for the carriage of the goods "at his own expense"; and A6 expressly mentions freight as one of the charges falling on the seller. In most cases, these articles will pose little problem.

Consider, however, the following situation. B sells to C on c.i.f. terms incorporating Incoterms 1990. B purchases a bill of lading from A covering goods conforming with B's on-sale to C. The bill of lading which B receives from A is marked "freight collect". Can B tender the bill of lading to C for the full contract price?

It is clear that C cannot be forced to pay the freight twice, once to B and once to the carrier. One solution would be for B to deduct from the invoice the amount of freight which C will need to pay the carrier before the goods are discharged, thus ensuring that B gets his price and that the carrier gets his freight – once.

It is not at all clear, however, that this device is available to the seller under Incoterms 1990 and if it is not, the seller runs the risk of being threatened with rejection of the contract by C if this suits C for commercial reasons. Articles A3 and A6 do not of themselves seem to prohibit this device explicitly and the UCP 500 expressly allow it by virtue of article 33(a). However, article A8 of the CIF incoterm arguably prohibits such a tender, providing as it does that the seller must tender a document which allows the buyer to claim the goods from the carrier at destination: a bill of lading marked "freight collect" arguably does not allow the buyer, without more, to claim the goods from the carrier at destination.

Appropriate drafting in the contract of sale will help resolve disputes which might arise where the seller tenders a "freight collect bill". It would be in the interests of the buyer to stipulate that the seller will only tender bills of lading which do not indicate that freight has yet to be be paid or, if such bills are tendered, then the invoice must make an appropriate deduction from the price.

III Route

Article A3 imposes on the seller the duty to make a contract of carriage "to the named port of destination by the usual route." Again, article A8 stipulates that the document tendered must be "for the agreed port of destination." Four points need to be made.

First, again here, it is clear that the CIF incoterm would be quite inappropriate for a contract for the sale of goods of which the buyer intends to take control at an inland depot. The incoterm to choose would be the CIP term, which at A3 provides that the seller must contract for the carriage of the goods "to the agreed point at the named place of destination."

Secondly, the contract of carriage tendered must provide for discharge <u>only</u> at the port stipulated for in the contract of sale. Thus where the destination port agreed in the contract of sale is only one of the ports allowed as discharge ports by the bill of lading, the seller is in breach of his obligation to tender documents for the agreed destination[18].

Thirdly, a seller is not in breach of his duty to contract for carriage by the usual route simply by virtue of the fact that the bill of lading allows the carrier to deviate. Under most carriage regimes, the carrier can only deviate for reasonable cause[19] and such a contract of carriage becomes a "usual" contract of carriage for the purposes of Incoterms. On the other hand, where the sale contract expressly stipulates for the direct shipment of the goods, the tender of a bill of lading allowing deviation would be a breach of the contract of sale[20].

Finally, when article A3 requires the seller to procure a contract of carriage "by the usual route" and A8 requires him to provide the buyer with the "usual transport document", does this mean that the seller is in breach if he tenders a bill of lading giving the carrier a liberty to tranship the goods onto a vessel other than that on which the goods were first shipped?

Transhipment and clauses giving the carrier a liberty to tranship are very "usual", particularly in the carriage of goods in containers. The danger from the buyer's point of view is that the bill of lading may go beyond giving the carrier a liberty to tranship and also seek to limit his liability to that part of the carriage performed on the initial ship or on ships in the ownership or under the management of the carrier. In this situation, the buyer may find himself bearing the risk of transit loss from the point of initial shipment, yet without any effective means of recovery against the initial carrier. Can the buyer now recover against the seller for breach of his physical and documentary duties under articles A3 and A8 of the CIF incoterm? It would appear that the answer is likely to be that the seller is not in breach[21], at any rate unless the buyer has taken care expressly to stipulate in the contract of sale for direct shipment[22].

IV The discharge of the goods

Article A8 states:

"This document (for example, a negotiable bill of lading, a non-negotiable sea waybill or an inland waterway document) must ... enable the buyer to claim the goods from the carrier at destination and, unless otherwise agreed, enable the buyer to sell the goods in transit by the transfer of the document to a subsequent buyer (the negotiable bill of lading) or by notification to the carrier."

This part of A8 goes directly to the nature of the document tendered as a key to the warehouse and raises the issue as to what type of transport document can be tendered by the seller to the buyer.

The article identifies two separate aspects of the "key" tendered by the seller to the buyer: it must allow the buyer access to the goods and it must, unless otherwise agreed, allow the buyer to transfer that right of access through the transfer of the document. Clearly a bill of lading would satisfy both requirements of article A8 if it is made out to the shipper's or the consignee's order, appropriately endorsed in full or in blank to the ultimate buyer if the goods have been sold while in transit.

However, difficulties arise where the document tendered by the seller provides the buyer with the right of access to the goods but not with the power of transfer. Thus, for example, what if the seller tenders a sea waybill, a bill of lading made out to the buyer without it being "to order", or a ship's delivery order acknowledging the buyer's right to delivery on discharge. All these documents clearly give the party for the time named as consignee[23] a right of access to the goods; none of them grant the buyer the power of transferring that right through transfer of the document. The upshot is that tender of such documents under the CIF incoterm would put the seller in breach "unless otherwise agreed." Where sellers expect to tender such a document, the documents clause in the contract of sale needs to be appropriately drafted, making it clear that the seller performs his documentary duties through tender of a bill of lading **or** a sea waybill[24] **or** a ship's delivery order. A failure to do so may catch the seller unawares where a buyer who is no longer interested in the goods, or in the goods at the contract price, puts the seller in breach and threatens to cancel the contract.

Conclusion

Contracts of sale which fail to clarify the type of contract of carriage which the seller must tender to the buyer cause unnecessary disputes. The mere incorporation of Incoterms 1990 into a contract of sale does not completely satisfy the commercial need for clarity and precision. While Incoterms 1990 provide an excellent agenda for traders concluding a contract of sale, that agenda needs to be filled in by appropriately drafted clauses in the body of the express contract itself.

Notes

1   Sale of Goods Act 1979, section 32(2).

2   Thus, for example, Bimchemvoybill bill of lading describes itself as a document "to be used for shipments under the Bimchemvoy charter"; the reverse page of the bill of lading is relatively short, incorporating most of its contractual terms from the charterparty with which it is intended to be used.

3   Precisely the same issue arises under the UCP 500, Article 25 of which does not clarify whether banks are to accept only "charterparty bills" properly so called, or also bills of lading which seek to incorporate terms from a charterparty.

4   In the absence of such a clause, the English courts would be likely to shy away from imposing such a duty: see Finska Cellulosaforeningen v. Westfield Paper Co Ltd [1940] 4 All E.R. 473 but cf. SIAT di dal Ferro v. Tradax Overseas SA [1980] 1 Lloyd's Rep. 53. The point discussed in the text is also referred to in Chapters 2 and 8 of this book.

5   A matter to which we shall return when dealing with the discharge of the goods.

6   Hansson v. Hamel & Horley (1922) 10 Ll.L Rep. 199 and 507. The contract pre-dates the first version of Incoterms, but it is submitted that the position would be the same in a contract incorporating Incoterms.

7   Or his insurer if, through a further mismatch between the sale and insurance contracts, the insurance policy is point-to-point.

8   See, for example, clause 10 of Form No. 100, the standard CIF contract for the sale of feeding stuffs in bulk issued by the Grain and Feed Trade Association.

9   Kleinjan & Holst N.V. Rotterdam v. Bremer Handelsgessellschaft m.b.H. [1972] 2 Lloyd's Rep. 11.

10   In The Ballenita and BP Energy [1992] 2 Lloyd's Rep. 455, the Commercial Court in London read a very wide power of substitution into a very short clause in the contract of sale stating the seller's duty of delivery as "CIF basis by M/T "TBN" or sub."

11   Re Keighley Maxtead & Co. and Bryant Durant & Co. (No.2) (1894) 70 L.T. 155.

12   The Wilomi Tanana [1993] 2 Lloyd's Rep. 41.

13   The Galatia [1980] 1 Lloyd's Rep. 453. See also, to similar effect, article 31(ii) of the UCP 500.

14   A bill of lading bearing a standard statement that the goods have been received for shipment but also carrying a later notation giving the date of actual shipment would constitute good tender under article A4 of the CIF incoterm. This would be in line with article 23(a)(ii) of the UCP 500.

15   Since the Sale and Supply of Goods Act 1994, section 15A of the Sale of Goods Act 1979 allows the seller to avoid rejection if "the breach is so slight that it would be unreasonable for [the buyer] to reject [the goods]." It is suggested that it is unlikely that this new section will be held to restrict the buyer's right to reject documents and goods in a c.i.f. sale where the bill of lading tendered is dated outside the contract period. In terms of sub-section 2 of section 15A itself, the section will not apply if "a contrary intention appears in, or is to be implied from, the contract."

16   Brown, Jenkinson & Co. v. Dalton (Percy)(London) [1957] 2 Lloyd's Rep. 1.

17   Kwei Tek Chao v. British Traders and Shippers [1954] 1 Lloyd's Rep. 16.

18   SIAT di dal Ferro v. Tradax Overseas SA [1980] 1 Lloyd's Rep. 53.

19   See, for example, Article IV.4 of the Hague-Visby Rules, which allows the carrier to deviate "in saving or attempting to save life or property at sea or any reasonable deviation."

20   Bergerco v. Vegoil [1984] 1 Lloyd's Rep. 440.

21   See Soproma v. Marine & Animal By-Products [1966] 1 Lloyd's Rep. 367: incoterm were not incorporated into the contract of sale here, but the contract of sale was on c.i.f. terms.

22   If payment is to be by letter of credit, the buyer may still find, somewhat to his surprise and possibly to his disadvantage, that payment has been made against a bill of lading allowing the carrier to tranship: see article 23(d)(ii) of the UCP 500.

23   Or attornee, as this party is commonly known in the context of ship's delivery orders.

24   This despite the fact that A8 expressly mentions a non-negotiable sea waybill as one of the documents that can be tendered by the seller to the buyer.

Incoterms and Documents

JEAN GUEDON

BART VAN DE VEIRE

1 Purpose and importance of documents

1.1 Purpose of documents named in Incoterms

Incoterms 1990 detail the main obligations of the seller and the buyer in an international contract of sale. The main elements are delivery, costs and transfer of risks. A review of the costs is given in the Guide to Incoterms[1]. The main categories of costs are:

• dispatch, carriage and delivery

• customs clearance for export and import

• services or assistance rendered by one party to the other in addition to what the assisting party is required to do under the respective trade term

• insurance.

Each of these costs signifies a service or act which is a necessary part of each party's performance under the contract of sale. The performance of the service must be evidenced by some kind of document. Incoterms give many details about the documents. Articles A1, A2 and B2, A3 (in CIF and CIP for insurance), A7 and B7, A8 and B8, A9 and B9, A10 and B10 are, completely or partly, directly or indirectly, related to documents. That makes 12 sections out of 20, which stresses the importance that Incoterms give to documents. Whether it is a written form or an electronic message, it is proof that a party has fulfilled its obligation or part of it.

The text itself of Incoterms 1990 mentions quite a few documents by their name, e.g. transport documents, but, in some cases, it refers to operations which necessitate documents without naming them. As an example, customs formalities are not a document, but they require, to be carried out, at least a declaration on a regular form. The Introduction to Incoterms, which underlines peculiar points, and the Guide, which develops comments about the terms, add other documents.

1.2   Types of documents named in Incoterms

1.2.1   Documents named in the text of Incoterms

In the text, article A1 mentions the commercial invoice. Articles A2 and B2 relate to customs documents. In the "C"-terms, documents of insurance are indicated in article A3. Articles A7 and B7, referring to notices that each party must give to the other, are quite important because if neglected by the parties (as sometimes happens), this could constitute a breach of contract. Except in EXW, article A8 of all terms mentions the transport documents by name; it must be noted that, in the previous versions of Incoterms, only the sea carriage documents were mentioned specifically but in the 1990 version, other transport documents are specified. Article B9 refers to preshipment inspection which is always evidenced by a document. Finally, articles A10 and B10 indicate the assistance that a party must give the other for obtaining documents.

1.2.2   Documents named in the Introduction

Among the documents mentioned in the Introduction[2] to the text of Incoterms is the charterparty. In the text of Incoterms itself, it is referred to only in article A8 of CFR and CIF, although it can be used in connection with any term, except, of course, EXW.

1.2.3   Documents mentioned in the Guide

All the above-mentioned documents are naturally mentioned in the Guide[3] but since this is more detailed, reference is also made to other documents such as the certificate of origin, the health certificate or the clean report of findings[4]. Even so, not all the documents used in practice are mentioned in Incoterms, the Introduction or the Guide, given that each country has its own requirements, e.g. for customs formalities.

The next paragraph will detail the documents named in Incoterms and give some practical tips about each of them. The use of Incoterms in the new version is easy for lawyers; it is not always the case for traders, who often have their operations performed by freight forwarders but would like to understand what is being done on their behalf.

2 Documents named in Incoterms

2.1 Commercial documents

The first document mentioned is the **commercial invoice** (article A1). Of course, the person most interested in this document is the buyer[5], but the document is also necessary, in most countries, if not all of them, for customs clearance. A proforma invoice will not be accepted, except temporarily in a few cases. It is also requested for other operations such as documentary credits.

The seller must also provide **any evidence of conformity** which might be required by the contract of sale (article A1). This can relate to the seller's obligations under article A9, viz. weighing, counting or packing. In some EC countries, since there are no longer customs formalities and the seller generally would not want to give the carrier a commercial invoice, another document is commonly used, which could be named "delivery voucher", to check the content of the vehicle on arrival. In fact, such document looks very much like an invoice without the price and a packing list.

Proof of delivery (articles A8 and B8) must be provided; if the transport document is not provided as proof of delivery, such proof can be of any type, e.g. dock receipt, FCR (Forwarding agent Certificate of Receipt), etc..

As to the **contract of sale** (articles B1 and others), its importance cannot be over-emphasised. Strictly speaking, it is not a document, since a contract is an agreement (which may be verbal or in writing), but such agreement is evidenced by a document that is commonly referred to as the contract of sale. Although a study of sale contracts is beyond the purpose of this book, it must still be stressed that the chosen incoterm is to be stipulated in this contract. If some elements relating to the delivery need clarification, reference must be made to the incoterm specified in the contract of sale and to any addition to such term.

2.2 Transport documents

Incoterms mention the **contract of carriage** (articles A3 and B3) and the **transport document** (articles A8 and B8). This document is very important since it is a receipt for the goods, evidence of the terms of the contract of carriage, occasionally a document giving instructions as to the collection of freight or other matters and sometimes a means of transferring rights to the goods. Depending upon the chosen incoterm, it can also be evidence of delivery under the contract of sale.

Close attention will be paid to the sea transport documents because this mode of carriage is subject to particular rules and customs quite different to those that will be found in the other modes of transport. Furthermore Incoterms 1990 contain two documents unknown to Incoterms 1980 which require a special development.

The most commonly used document in sea transport is the **marine bill of lading**, or **ocean bill of lading**. Issued by the shipowner, carrier, the master or their agent, the bill of lading has three functions.

1) The bill of lading serves as a receipt for the goods

As a receipt it will contain the description and quantity of the goods. If the goods were not received by the ship in apparent good order, the bill of lading will also contain the necessary notations to describe the state of the goods accordingly.

The bill of lading will normally confirm the receipt of goods on board. However, sometimes the carrier will issue a bill of lading simply confirming receipt prior to the loading of the goods on board: in this case, the bill of lading will state, either in the printed form or by special stamp, that the goods have been "received" by the carrier in a stated quantity and condition. Such a bill of lading serves as a receipt of the goods by the carrier, but does not serve as proof that the goods have actually been loaded on board. In the case of an FOB sale, it is clear that tender of such a bill of lading puts the seller in breach of his duty to deliver the goods "free on board" the nominated vessel, at any rate where the bill of lading does not also carry the date of actual shipment of the goods. Again, with CIF and CFR sales, the seller must tender a document which is "dated within the period agreed for shipment", which must mean that a bill of lading merely giving the date on which the goods have been received for shipment would be a bad tender under these incoterms.

2) The bill of lading is evidence of the terms of the contract of carriage concluded between shipper and carrier

The bill of lading may provide evidence of all the terms of the contract of carriage, or may refer to them in another document (the so-called shortform or blank back bill of lading) or simply a bill of lading referring to a booking note or a charterparty.

3) The bill of lading is a document of title

This means that the carrier is bound to give the goods on arrival at the discharge port only to the holder of a bill of lading. Delivery of the goods to a non-holder of the bill of lading exposes the carrier to an action by the holder of the bill of lading. Moreover, during the period of transit of the goods, the bill of lading symbolises the goods, and the holder may sell the goods even at this time simply by endorsing and delivering the bill of lading.

4) The issuer of the document

It is important to refer here to the definition of a carrier as described in the introduction to the FCA term in Incoterms 1990 : "carrier" means any person who, in a contract of carriage, undertakes to perform or to procure the performance of carriage by rail, road, sea, air, inland waterway or by a combination of such modes. Consequently he will assume the liability of a carrier and establish the carrier-type documents.

In other words the capacity to act as carrier is not exclusively for a shipowner or a vessel operating carrier. A freight forwarder offering the same contract of carriage, assuming the carrier's liability and issuing transport documents accordingly, is to be considered a carrier as well.

A **sea waybill** has only the two first functions of the ocean bill of lading, i.e. it serves as a receipt of goods and is evidence of the terms of the contract of carriage. However, it is not a document of title. As a consequence the consignee named in the sea waybill only needs to identify himself in order to take delivery of the goods.

1) Limitations of the sea waybill

Since it is not a document of title to the goods, the goods cannot be sold en route through transfer of the document. If parties wish to retain that option, they must opt for shipment under an ocean or marine bill of lading.

The CIF & CFR terms explicitly require that the document tendered "...must ... enable the buyer to claim the goods from the carrier at destination and, **unless otherwise agreed,** enable the buyer to sell the goods in transit by the transfer of the document to the buyer (the negotiable bill of lading) or by notification to the carrier." Now although the sea waybill is expressly mentioned as one of the documents which can be tendered under the CIF and CFR terms, the requirement cited above makes it clear that such a document can only be tendered where the parties have expressly agreed on such tender in the contract of sale. Without such agreement, tender of a sea waybill would not conform to the CFR or CIF terms because the document does not facilitate the sale of the goods in transit, either by transfer or by notification to the carrier. Alternatively, the parties should choose to contract on CPT or CIP terms, neither of which make a similar requirement to that cited above.

2) Advantages of the sea waybill

The advantage of the sea waybill lies in the fact that presentation of the document by the consignee is not required in order to obtain delivery of the cargo in the port of discharge.

In a number of short-sea and other fast shipping trades, the sea waybill is therefore very popular, because it avoids delays to ships and cargo in the port of discharge whenever consignees have to wait for the arrival of the bills of lading before they can take delivery of the goods.

A further sign of the increased use of the sea waybill has been the introduction of a separate article in the recent revision of ICC Uniform Customs and Practices for Documentary Credits (UCP 500) describing the conditions under which banks will accept a sea waybill required by a letter of credit[6].

3) The carriage regime applicable to a sea waybill

The rules generally applicable to the classic bill of lading, viz. the Hague Rules or Hague-Visby Rules are, in most countries where they are in force, not compulsorily applicable to the sea waybill. Carriers using sea waybills, however, frequently make the Hague or

Hague-Visby rules applicable by incorporating them in the terms and conditions of their contract.

On the other hand, the Hamburg Rules apply in their own terms to any transport document covering ocean carriage (or a carriage consisting partly of an ocean carriage), including the sea waybill.

In the absence of any compulsory rules governing the sea waybills, the Comité Maritime International adopted in 1990 the CMI Uniform Rules for Sea Waybills. Where these Rules are incorporated into a contract of carriage not covered by a bill of lading, the contract of carriage will be subject to the same regime which would have been applicable had the contract been covered by a bill of lading. The effect is to extend by contract the documents to which the Hague and Hague-Visby Rules apply[7]. The Rules also allow for the entry on a sea waybill of a clause preventing the shipper from altering the carrier's delivery instructions. Without such a clause, the shipper could deprive the consignee of his right to delivery from the carrier through the simple expedient of altering the carrier's delivery instructions before discharge. A "right of control" clause protects the consignee from such an event by passing the right of controlling the goods from the shipper to the consignee.

The **Multimodal Transport bill of lading** differs from the ocean bill of lading in the kind of carriage the carrier has agreed upon.

The Multimodal Transport bill of lading evidences the contract between shipper and carrier, here called the Multimodal Transport Operator (MTO), for the carriage of goods involving at least two different modes of transport. The MTO issuing a Multimodal Transport bill of lading is responsible for the goods from the time he receives them until the time he delivers them at destination.

The fact that we use the term Multimodal Transport bill of lading implies that at least two of the three functions of the traditional bill of lading apply also to the Multimodal Transport bill of lading.

1)   The Multimodal bill of lading serves as a receipt for the goods

The receipt of the cargo by the carrier does not necessarily mean that the goods have actually been shipped on board the vessel. Receipt of the goods may mean only the loading on board any vehicle or even a simple handing over of the cargo to the carrier at any inland terminal.

2) The Multimodal bill of lading is evidence of the terms of the carriage concluded between shipper and carrier

There is considerable doubt as to whether the Multimodal Transport Document is a document of title. While there is no doubt that such a document is acceptable to the banks in the circumstances envisaged by article 26 of the Uniform Customs and Practice for Documentary Credits, the better view seems to be that it cannot transfer control of the goods while in transit through the simple endorsement of the document.

3) The carriage regime applicable to a Multimodal Transport bill of lading

With regard to the liability of the Multimodal Transport Operator (MTO), the United Nations adopted the UN Convention on International Multimodal Transport of Goods of 1980, (the MT Convention). Pending the entry into force of the MT Convention, UNCTAD, in close cooperation with the ICC, set up a joint UNCTAD/ICC working group to elaborate provisions for Multimodal Transport Documents based on the Hague Rules and the Hague-Visby Rules as well as the then existing documents such as the FIATA Combined Transport bill of lading and the ICC Uniform Rules for a Combined Transport Document (ICC Publication 298). This resulted in the UNCTAD/ICC rules for Multimodal Transport Documents (ICC Publication 481), which are intended to avoid a multiplicity of different requirements governing such transportation and to provide a transport contract with a uniform legal form. The new rules entered into force on January 1, 1992.

FIATA, who actively participated in the elaboration of the UNCTAD/ICC Rules on Multimodal Transport Documents, was the first to work out a new Multimodal Transport bill of lading which was in accordance with the new rules.

On August 4, 1993, the ICC confirmed that the Negotiable FIATA Multimodal Transport Bill of Lading conformed to the requirements of the UNCTAD/ICC Rules for Multimodal Transport Documents and was allowed in evidence of this fact to bear the ICC logo.

It is obvious that freight forwarders who issue a Negotiable FIATA Multimodal Transport bill of lading enter into a Multimodal Transport contract and assume responsibility for the performance thereof as a carrier. In other words, they become a carrier.

As a consequence, FIATA ruled that the national organisations distributing the Negotiable FIATA Multimodal Transport bill of lading[8] – among their members freight forwarders – must see to it that the carrier's liability which follows from the issuing of the FBL, is properly insured, either through an individual policy or through a collective policy (e.g. Belgium).

If the seller and the buyer have decided that the place of delivery is not going to be a ship's rail but a carrier's terminal (inland or in the port of loading), it is obvious that the appropriate incoterm will be either FCA or CPT/CIP, depending on whether the buyer or the seller should contract for carriage.

Under these terms, it is absolutely clear that a Multimodal Transport bill of lading should qualify as an appropriate transport document which the seller must provide to the buyer at the latter's expense[9].

The **inland waterway document** can be of any type. Quite often it ·is a charterparty. There are also **inland waterway waybills.** On the Rhine and adjacent rivers, a **Rhenan bill of lading** is commonly used.

The other documents, namely the **air waybill,** the **railway consignment note** and the **road consignment note** (articles A8 and B8) have a number of points in common with bills of lading and with each other, but also differ from bills of lading in important respects. In common with bills of lading, these documents also perform the role of a receipt and the role of evidence of the terms of the contract of carriage[10]. On the other hand, these documents are not documents of title and are therefore never negotiable. The obligation of the carrier is to hand over the goods to the consignee named in the document without any need for presentation. A copy of the document is always handed over to the shipper[11], and this leaves with him the right, at any rate under the contract of carriage, to dispose of the goods after they have been shipped, i.e. he can change the destination, or the consignee, or even order the return of the goods to their point of departure.

This power of the seller, as shipper under the contract of carriage, to give instructions to the carrier as to the disposal of the goods, presents serious risks to the buyer who can thereby be deprived, as against the carrier, of his right to delivery of the goods[12]. Mindful of this risk, the ICC advises buyers under "C"-terms[13] to insist in their contract of sale on the tender of a document containing a "non-disposal" clause.

While the wisdom of this advice is clear, it should be said that the risk to the buyer of the seller giving the carrier different delivery instructions can be over-estimated. Where the seller has yet to be paid, either directly by the buyer or indirectly by a bank under a letter of credit, it is extremely unlikely that he will wish to alter the carrier's delivery instructions. Even where the seller has already been paid, but the goods have been shipped, the exercise by the seller of his right, as shipper, to alter deliver instructions involves the handing over of the document to the carrier – a surrender which is unlikely to be desirable to the seller. The risk is at its greatest where the buyer pays the seller before the goods are actually shipped, as sometimes happens in the sale of equipment on cash advances. On one view, the buyer has no one to blame but himself in such circumstances. Whether or not this view is too harsh, the fact that the buyer has been deprived of his right to delivery of the goods *as against the carrier* does not mean that he necessarily has no remedy against the seller under the contract of sale.

The **air waybill** is drafted on a universal form established in 1983 by IATA (International Air Transport Association), which is also used by non-IATA companies. There are three originals, one for the shipper, another for the carrier and the last one for the consignee. Practically all countries have adopted the Warsaw Convention which regulates air transport. The transport document is commonly issued by a freight forwarder who acts as agent of the carrier. It is common practice that he is not chosen by the buyer when he has to contract for carriage, but by the seller, who, in the same time, has him to clear the goods for export.

The **railway consignment note** will be different in different areas of the world, but it must be noticed that the main area of international rail transport is Europe, and all European countries have adopted or are about to adopt the international convention

C.I.M. (Convention Internationale pour le transport des Marchandises par chemins de fer), which is also applicable to some adjacent countries. It must be underlined that the document for carriage can be used as a transit document in EC and EFTA countries[14]. A new form has been created, implemented on 1, January, 1993. The document is issued by the carrier upon a declaration of the shipper who is responsible for the information he gives. Though it is used as a transit document, it does not fall under article A6 of Incoterms, because the transit function is only complementary to the main function of carriage document.

The same kind of convention exists in European countries and some adjacent countries for road carriage. It is the CMR (Convention internationale pour le transport des Marchandises par Route)[15]. The **road consignment note** is the same in all those countries, but it cannot be used as a transit document. For transit between EC and EFTA countries, the EC form will be used (Single Administrative Document)[16], and for transit in other countries, it will be a TIR document (TIR: Transit International Routier). The transport document is issued by the carrier upon a declaration of the shipper who is responsible for the information he gives. Of course, the CMR consignment note is not used in other areas of the world, but each country or association of countries has its own form. It will be ruled by articles A8 and B8.

It is obvious that the **Multimodal Transport Document** envisaged by UNCTAD/ICC Publication 481 can apply to any mode of transport including at least two types of different carriage and what has been said about the Multimodal Transport bill of lading is applicable to such a document. This kind of document will develop more and more. First, air and rail carriages generally need precarriage and on-carriage. Secondly, as stressed in the Introduction to Incoterms as well as in the Guide, there is a general trend towards arrival contracts of sale, and consequently a development of the "D"-terms for which this document is particularly adapted.

2.3 Custom documents

Customs and transit are expressly referred to in articles A2 and B2, and A6 and B6; and implicitly in A10 and B10.

Articles A2 and B2 do not expressly name a document: they refer expressly to the seller's duty to "carry out all customs formalities." However, as indicated earlier, the manner in which this duty is performed is necessarily documentary and the main document in use here is the **declaration.** This document is always required for export as well as for import, other than in trade inside the EC. As already mentioned, in trade between the EC and EFTA countries, a common form of declaration is used, the Single Administrative Document (SAD). The declaration commonly contains a reference to the delivery terms upon which the contract of sale has been concluded and it should be mentioned that some countries, mainly developing ones, refuse to allow reference to the newer terms designed for use with container traffic. In fact, the practice is to contract under a term that will regulate the commercial relations between seller and buyer such as FCA, CPT or CIP, but then to give FOB, CFR or CIF as the delivery term on the declaration.

Export or import licences are used in practically all countries but to varying degrees. Since they are not always known under this name, the text of Incoterms mentions any **official authorisation.** This generic term would include new documents now in use for trade within the EC, documents to which reference will be made below. In EXW and FAS terms, the buyer must obtain the export licence. He will use for that purpose the services of a local freight forwarder in the seller's country. In most cases, if not all of them, this freight forwarder will need the help of – even if only by way of obtaining information from – the seller. This is part of the assistance that the seller must render the buyer, at the latter's risk and expense, according to article A2. Conversely, under DEQ and DDP terms, the buyer will render the seller the same kind of assistance for obtaining the import licence, according to article B2.

The **transit document** is regulated in a general manner by articles A6 or B6, sometimes by B10. When drafted on the Single Administrative form, this transit document is automatically issued when drafting the export declaration and can be considered as a mere complement of this declaration. In such a case, articles A2 and B2 will be relevant. It must be added, since some products are still subject to customs formalities inside the EC, that the text of Incoterms mentions "transit through another country", which excludes the countries of departure and arrival.

The Guide also mentions the **certificate of origin** and the **health certificate**[17]. The first is required for importation but issued in the country of origin or shipment. The latter is required at times for export and at others for import. According to the Guide, when the party in charge of the customs clearance cannot obtain them directly, the other party must render assistance in obtaining them, which falls under article A10 of Incoterms.

The Guide could not mention all the documents that can be issued for export or import formalities in another country and are necessary for clearance but it mentions certificates, consular invoices, permits, authorizations, legalisation, which are included in the clearance operations and thus should fall under articles A2 or B2, but sometimes could as well be relevant to articles A10 or B10. The distinction between these two sets of articles is not always very easy. According to the Guide[18], articles A2 and B2 are intended to cover the cases in which one party must carry out the customs clearance in the other party's country, i.e. in EXW and FAS, DEQ and DDP terms. Other documents, such as the certificates of origin or of health, are not, strictly speaking, customs documents but administrative documents which properly fall under articles A10 and B10. Thus, for example, for some goods a health certificate will be issued in the country of export, with another being issued in the country of import. In either case, whether the document falls under articles A2 and B2 or A10 and B10, the result is the same: one party must render assistance to the other for obtaining the documents at the latter one's risk and cost. Equally, though it does not occur very often, documents issued in the country of import can be necessary for the seller to carry out customs formalities for export, e.g. in the trade of goods subject to control of final destination, and will fall under article B2.

2.4   Insurance documents

These are mentioned in CIF and CIP terms. The **insurance policy** is the document evidencing the **insurance contract** (articles A3 of CIF and CIP). It is a detailed review of the cover guaranteed by the insurer. There is no universal form and each country has its own kind of form and even of style. Since insurance is dealt with in Chapter 5 of this book, suffice it here to say that insurance documents are of great significance for the parties, both in their own right and in connection with the letter of credit. Rather than tender an insurance policy, Incoterms allow the seller to tender other **evidence of insurance cover**[19], which is a short form of the policy giving the main elements of the risks covered.

It should be noted that the insurance cover which the seller is required to procure for the buyer under articles A3(b) of CIF and CIP may not cover all the perils which may befall the goods since the seller's duty, failing express stipulation, is only to obtain the minimum cover of the Institute Cargo Clauses. Thus it may well be in the buyer's interests to take out insurance on his own account for losses not covered by the policy which the seller is required to tender by Incoterms. This is even more obviously the case, of course, where the seller is under no obligation to effect insurance. In these circumstances, Incoterms assist the buyer by imposing on the seller a duty to provide the buyer, upon request, with the necessary information for procuring insurance[20].

2.5   **Other documents**

Article A7 of all incoterms mentions a number of details of which the seller must give **notice to the buyer**. Similarly, article B7 mentions a number of facts of which the buyer must give **notice to the seller.** Too often, parties do not give enough importance to these notices; yet the consequences of not giving such notices may well be serious. Thus, the Guide to Incoterms explains[21] that the failure to carry out these formalities may constitute a breach of the contract of such severity as to entitle the other party to cancel the contract. Moreover, Incoterms make it clear in terms that where the buyer is in breach of article B7, the buyer will bear the risk of loss occurring prior to the delivery of the goods and will bear the costs incurred as a result of the breach, at any rate where the goods have been "clearly set aside or otherwise identified as the contract goods"[22].

The text of article A7 reads that there must be a **sufficient notice.** The Guide indicates that the notice can be sent by cable, telex, etc., but there is no guidance as to the time beyond which the notice will be deemed insufficient. Though it does not apply directly to Incoterms, it may be of interest to point out that under the French "ventes maritimes", i.e. sales of goods carried by sea[23], the period allowed for a similar notice is 24 hours.

Checking operations of article A9 are not documents but they can be ascertained by documents which most times will fall under the evidence of conformity of article A1. On the other hand where special pre-shipment inspection is requested by the buyer, as sometimes happens in the sale of commodities, it is the buyer who bears the costs thus incurred.

The **pre-shipment inspection** mentioned in article B9 is frequently required in circumstances where there is a gap of trust between exporter and importer or between their respective governments. Inspections are carried out by such organizations as Lloyd's or the Bureau Veritas and the common use of these inspections does not attract warm support among European shippers. Of course, an inspection is not a document, but the inspector issues a document which is sometimes named "certificate of inspection" and, at any rate when the inspection is positive, a "clean report of findings". Where the assistance of the seller is necessary for the performance of these inspections, the seller must give such assistance under article A10.

All the documents that are required in international sales cannot be named in Incoterms. There are such papers as the certificate of boycott for import of goods in Arab countries or the Rabbi's certificate for import of foodstuffs into Israel. And the choice is particularly rich in the field of animal or vegetable products. But all of them can be classified in one of the main categories that are given above and fall under one of the sections of the text of Incoterms.

3   Changes in documents inside the single market

3.1   Suppression of documents

The suppression of the customs formalities inside the EC is a general principle. As a general rule, the Single Administrative Document is no longer used in trade between Member States of the Community, but there are still some exceptions where it is used[24]. Customs formalities must be carried out for exchanges with overseas territories of EC countries as well as for goods subject to control of final destination. If some documents have been suppressed, others have been created. Existing documents are still used but not in the same manner. The transit by sea and air inside the EC is maintained though simplified.

3.2 New documents in EC trade

Before 1993, it was decided by the EC that, at the opening of the Single Market, information which had been given in customs declarations should be provided by trade operators for statistical purpose or for the regulation of the payment of VAT. First, consignors and consignees were to provide periodically in "Summary Tables" statistical information regarding the delivery terms upon which they had traded, through specific reference to one of the terms included in Incoterms. Second, EC Sales Lists indicating supplies and acquisitions, according to the new wording of EC, were to be periodically established, independently of the regular forms required by each state for the payment of VAT.

It must be noted that payment of VAT was not regulated in the same manner in all EC countries. As regards goods coming from another country, it was always controlled by the customs service, but it was not necessarily collected by this service. Then, as regards the two new formalities described above for use in the Single Market, the Commission of the EC specified the information required but left it to the different states to choose the manner of collection and the frequency of the drawing up of Sales Lists, so long as this did not exceed three months. Moreover, the administrative authorities concerned were also allowed to effect the Summary Tables and the Sales Lists in the same formality. Thus France has chosen to use one form for both.

The significant point for Incoterms is that these new documents are not documents which the seller or buyer are obliged to provide to each other under Incoterms. They are neither an official authorisation nor a document that could be required by a party for exportation, importation or transit.

Another new document is awaited, concerning products subject to control of the final destination, commonly called strategic products. The EC Commission issued in 1992 an indicative regulation but it contained only general principles. The problem was that on the one hand there were forms used both in the EC and in other countries, while on the other there were other forms for similar goods used only in some member states of the EC. The purpose of the EC Commission in this regard was to create a common simplified form for the trading of such goods intra-Community. At the time of writing, this form has not yet been issued.

In the meantime, the absence of a new form does not cause too much of a problem because strategic goods are the only trade for which customs formalities are still necessary in intracommunity trade. A Single Administrative Document must be filled in and accompanied by an export licence or some other document such as the Gl or LIDIS licence. One document was recently created: the Schengen licence which can be used in the EC but only between the countries which signed the Schengen agreement, namely Belgium, France, Germany, Italy, Luxemburg, Netherlands, Portugal and Spain.

3.3   Fiscal matters; bonds and guarantees

It should be stressed, though, that the suppression of the customs declaration in intra-Community trade has brought some problems that are not easy to solve. Customs matters have become fiscal matters and, as such, cannot be solved by a general rule drawn from Incoterms, since, if there was a harmonization of customs procedures, there is none of fiscal procedures. Each country is free to apply its own rules if the decision of EC authorities is respected. That is the reason why Incoterms should not deal with fiscal matters.

But there are cases in which Incoterms can help. A new document has been created at the opening of the single market for the transit inside EC of goods subject to excise duty like tobacco, alcohol, etc. This operation must be guaranteed by a bond, and somebody has to pay for this bond. Since it is a fiscal matter, each country may establish its own rules, and Incoterms cannot give an answer as to who has to bear the cost of the bond. But, insofar as the bond is linked with an accompanying document, Incoterms can say who is in charge of the document and consequently bears the cost of the bond connected with it.

3.4   Transit

Transit through a non-EC country illustrates well one of the changes brought about by the Single Market. For a shipment of goods from Germany to Italy through Austria, a transit document T2 is necessary since the goods are passing through a non-EC country. Before the opening of the Single Market, the operations of export and transit were made simultaneously, the transit being a mere complement of the export and there was one declaration for both formalities and it was paid for by the seller, except in EXW and FAS. Nowadays, there is no export clearance and, under "F"- and "C"-terms, according to article B6, the cost of the transit falls on the buyer. Of course, for practical reasons, it will be carried out by the seller, but in so doing he will have assisted the buyer with obtaining a document issued in the country of origin, and the cost of such assistance, according to article A10, falls on the buyer.

The same point can be illustrated through the following example. In the same situation as above, a transit document must be established for passing through Austria. This transit will be guaranteed by a bond and the cost of the bond will be borne by the so-called "principal" on the document. The principal will invoice the one who gave him the order to issue the transit form, i.e. the seller or the buyer according to the chosen incoterm; the invoice will cover both his own operations for issuance of the document as the price of the bond. In "F"- or "C"-terms, the charge for the transit is to the buyer's account. In fact, for practical reasons, it will be taken care of by the seller who is in the country of departure, but again, the seller will have given the buyer assistance in obtaining a document, the cost for which will fall on the buyer according to article A10.

In such cases, the charge for the document is ruled by articles A2 and A10 of all incoterms. It should not be too difficult to determine whether it is an official authorization or a document issued in the country of shipment and/or of origin or importation that may be required for the exportation and/or the importation, according to the chosen term.

3.5   New use of common documents

In the transit by sea or air between EC ports or airports, a document T2L was required. For simplification reasons, it has been suppressed and replaced by another procedure. The designation T2L is written for the products subject to this formality on the cargo manifest, which is a document required for the clearance of the ship or plane. Indeed both of them have to be cleared by customs on arrival and departure, and give a cargo manifest, that is, a list of the goods on board. This applies both to goods that will be discharged and to those which are in transit. Now since this formality concerns the carrier, Incoterms do not deal with it expressly. Incoterms concern the seller and the buyer, not the carrier. The question arises also as to who is to bear the cost of this procedure. One could say that it relates to the transit and must be ruled by articles A6 or B6 of the incoterms. But, on the other hand, the formality is carried out by the carrier and the extra cost will be included in the cost of the carriage. We can consider that it falls on the party that pays for the carriage.

As to the products of the CAP or Common Agricultural Policy, the result of the suppression of customs formalities has been quite paradoxical: it led to the suppression of documents. At the end of 1992, negative monetary compensatory amounts were re-established in the UK and Italy as the result of a devaluation. Since the customs formalities had to be eliminated a few months later, it was decided to use a document already existing, albeit for a different purpose, the so-called T5. But it became clear very soon that, with the suppression of border controls, there was nobody to scrutinize the use of this form. Thus the solution was the suppression of the T5, at least for that use, and the suppression of the compensatory amounts as well. They have been replaced by prices adapted to each country, according to a complex system, a mechanism which falls outside the orbit of Incoterms.

4 Chartering documents

4.1 Charterparties

In most legal systems the charterparty is not considered as a transport document to be tendered between traders, because chartering is not simply a contract for the carriage of goods by sea. The main object of this contract is the ship rather than the goods. However, the document which evidences the carriage of the goods shipped, even where shipped on a chartered vessel, i.e. the bill of lading, is of great importance between the parties to the contract of sale.

4.2 Charterparty bills of lading

Incoterms "C"- and "D"- specify that a transport document must be provided. Since the charterparty is not such a document, a bill of lading has to be issued. This is particularly important if the cargo is sold while at sea or if there is a letter of credit. Many charterparty forms contemplate the use of a particular type of bill of lading.

It is mentioned in Incoterms that, if a bill of lading refers to a charterparty, a copy of this charterparty should be provided. This was included in the text because of frauds on cargoes under charterparties sold while at sea. The duty to tender a copy of the charterparty raises practical problems. As a general rule, the seller, when he is the charterer, will not wish the buyer to know the details of the charterparty, except the necessary stipulations for discharging such as laydays and demurrage. First, he does not want the buyer to know the price of the carriage. Second, laydays for loading and discharging are often reversible. If, as in an actual case, the total number is six laydays, loading in one port has taken four days, two days are left to discharge in four ports, for commercial reasons, the seller would most certainly prefer that the buyer remains forever in ignorance of this! The seller will only let him know there are two laydays for discharging and the cost of demurrage. There are other reasons, but these seem to be the main ones.

However, the text of Incoterms specifies that, "if the transport document contains a reference to a charterparty, the seller must also provide a copy of this latter document"[25]. What can be considered as a reference to a charterparty? Some charterparties include types of bills of lading which often bear a code name in which one can sometimes recognise the type of the charterparty, but that seems to be too weak a reference to trigger the obligation to tender the charterparty.

It could be argued that where, in a particular trade, it is the custom that sellers do not tender a copy of the charterparty, then this special custom will supersede the express terms of Incoterms. However, it seems that there is no such custom when the cargo is sold while at sea. In such a case, the new buyer will not only ask for the bill of lading but also for other documents evidencing the existence of the cargo as well as its quality, quantity, stipulations about discharging, etc; and the proof that it is on board a vessel at sea. The charterparty can be considered as one of these documents. It must be remarked that, before "buying" the bill of lading, the future buyer will make a payment to obtain these documents, among which should be a copy of the charterparty.

Guidance was given at a meeting of the Working Party for the interpretation of Incoterms[26]. Only if the seller makes full reference to the charterparty must he produce the entire charterparty contract. Otherwise, the seller will at most provide the buyer information with respect to discharging such as demurrage and laytime provisions contained in the charterparty. This point is also discussed in Chapters 1 and 8 of this book.

But there are some disadvantages with the use of the charterparty bill of lading. The back of the bill of lading shows only general conditions, and, in order to prove that after the delivery at the port of departure in a "C"-term and the prepayment of the freight, the seller has no more obligation nor anything to pay, mainly in discharging operations, the face of the document is, quite often, full of so many explanations that the banker who examines the documents under a letter of credit is completely lost, and, sometimes refuses them or issues exceptions[27].

It must finally be added that, if the relations between the owner and the charterer are ruled by the charterparty, when a bill of lading is issued and transferred to a third party, the relations between the carrier and the third party bearer of the bill of lading are ruled by the Hague or Hague-Visby Rules if either of these conventions are applicable.

5 Conclusion

As outlined at the beginning of this chapter, the 1990 version of Incoterms gives more importance to documents than the previous versions. It is stressed in the Introduction to Incoterms that the reason for a re-draft only ten years after the previous version was to adapt the terms to the increasing use of EDI and also to new transportation techniques. Since one of the main purposes of EDI is to replace documents, it was necessary to detail those documents.

As to new transportation techniques, there are deep changes though the development of multimodal transport. New documents have been created and old documents will lose part of their importance, such as the marine bill of lading – which already was a fact – or the FIATA bill of lading, which was not mentioned in Incoterms but in UCP 400. There are new combinations of means of carriage, such as road and rail – which has existed for some time but is developing further – or containers and inland waterway carriage.

Furthermore, new economic areas are developing all over the world. The most important, so far, is the EC, but others come to birth, e.g. in North America. That brings a change in customs formalities, and, consequently, in customs documents.

Finally, the division of Incoterms into ten sections made it necessary to develop the number of documents mentioned in all the basic texts, i.e. the text itself, the Introduction and the Guide. Nobody can now fail to be aware who, seller or buyer, has to provide a document.

Notes

1   ICC Publication No. 461/90.

2   Incoterms 1990, ICC Publication No.460, p.13, para.15.

3   "Guide to Incoterms 1990", ICC Publication No.461/90.

4   "Guide to Incoterms 1990", op. cit., explanation to article A10 of most of the terms.

5   The commercial invoice must be "in conformity with the contract of sale".

6   UCP 500, ICC Publication No.500, article 24.

7   CMI Uniform Rules for Sea Waybills, article 4(i).

8   FIATA DOC 10/71/annex 1993-08-26.

9   See articles A8 in the FCA, CPT and CIP Incoterms 1990.

10   For obvious reasons, the distinction between "shipped" and "received for shipment" documents does not apply here.

11   Who can also use such documents under letters of credit, where the banks have agreed to open such letters on the strength of such documents.

12   This would not, of course, necessarily deprive the buyer of his remedies for non-delivery against the seller under the contract of sale.

13   See Incoterms, ICC Publication 460, at page 16.

14   The EFTA (European Free Trade Association) countries are Switzerland, Austria and Liechtenstein, Norway, Sweden, Finnland and Iceland.

15   The CMR was ratified at first by Austria, France, Italy, the Netherlands and Yugoslavia, then by Belgium, Bulgaria, Czechoslovakia, Denmark, Finland, both parts of Germany, Great Britain, Greece, Hungary, Luxembourg, Norway, Poland, Portugal, Roumania, Spain, Sweden, Switzerland and the USSR. However, the Convention applies in all cases where the point of departure or arrival is in one of these countries, e.g. for a carriage from France to Iran.

16   Two Conventions concluded with EFTA countries on May 20, 1987 (see 1987 O.J. No.L.134 p.2 and 1987 O.J. No.L.226 p.1 and EC Bull. No.5, points 2.1.53, 2.1.54) make possible the use of the Single Administrative Document in trade with them and simplifies transit procedures, cf. EC Com. 21st General Report at No.177 (1988).

17   See the explanation to article A10 of most of the Incoterms.

18   See Guide to Incoterms, pages 17, 24 and 27.

19   See Incoterms 1990, CIF, article A3.

20   See, for example, article A10 in FOB and CFR.

21   At page 37.

22   See Incoterms articles B5 and B6.

23   This law does not apply to international sales, which rather limits the utility of the law.

24   See endnote 16 above.

25   cf. article A8.

26   Working Party on Trade Terms, summary record, meeting of 4 May 1994.

27   See Chapter 4, Incoterms and the UCP 500.

Incoterms, EDI and Electronic Messaging

GUILLERMO JIMENEZ

1 Introductory – What is EDI?

In essence, electronic data interchange (EDI) allows one company's computer system to be connected to those of its trading partners via public or private networks. The difference between EDI and electronic mail (E-mail) or private computer networks is that EDI involves the transmission of standardized messages, like purchase orders and invoices, between two companies. Since message structures conform to an agreed standard, a company can use a single software program to dialogue with hundreds of different clients or suppliers.

EDI is thus the computer-to-computer transmission of electronic messages according to an agreed message standard, often in substitution for traditional paper documents that were previously mailed or sent by telefax.

In an era of increased global competition many companies are using EDI, which enables instantaneous transmission of business data, to help them cope with mountains of information, and ever-tighter deadlines. "Just-in-time" manufacturing, for example, with its premium on quick delivery, depends on EDI.

EDI has also been a key to the recent growth of electronic banking services, port and transport management, and commercial invoicing. Since an EDI message is transmitted instantly over a computer network, it allows for goods to be ordered and shipped much more quickly, allowing companies to save money on the maintenance of warehouses and inventory.

EDI lacks a fully functioning universal standard, although the United Nations' EDIFACT (EDI For Administration, Commerce and Trade) norm may eventually provide a solution by becoming the predominant standard. Other obstacles to EDI commonly cited include legal uncertainties, lack of awareness, and commercial resistance to this new way of doing business. Despite this, EDI use continues to grow.

2 How does EDI relate to Incoterms?

Since one of the principal applications of EDI technology in business has been in the transport sector, it became necessary to adapt incoterms for EDI practices. One of the innovations of Incoterms 1990, therefore, was to provide for the validity of electronic messages. Thus, in articles A8 and B8 of Incoterms 1990, "Proof of delivery, transport document or equivalent electronic message", it is provided that: "Where the seller and the buyer have agreed to communicate electronically, the [usual document] may be replaced by an equivalent electronic data interchange (EDI) message."

It should first be noted that EDI is only acceptable when both parties have previously agreed to accept electronic messages in lieu of other forms of communication. One party cannot, therefore, unilaterally begin to communicate electronically, or otherwise assume that an electronic message would be acceptable to the other party, without having first obtained the other party's assent.

While an international sale of goods may require a continual exchange of information between the two parties, much of which could be transmitted electronically (i.e., offers, acceptances, notices, information), Incoterms 1990 only refer to EDI in the context of documents constituting proof of delivery. With the exception of EXW, all incoterms require the seller to provide the buyer with a document evidencing proof of delivery. With many of these documents, such as freight receipts, carrier's receipts, liner way-bills, and other forms of non-negotiable documents, there should be no impediment to replacement of the paper document by an electronic message (provided both parties have agreed to adopt such a system). On the other hand, where a bill of lading – a unique type of document due to its negotiable status – is used, special problems for EDI arise.

A bill of lading (unlike waybills and the other documents just mentioned) not only constitutes proof of delivery of goods but also constitutes legal control over the goods, or as is commonly said, "the bill of lading represents the goods". Thus, only the holder of the "original" bill of lading is entitled to claim the goods from the carrier at destination. The concept of a paper "original" is not easily transposed into an electronic context, where there are no "originals". The development of an electronic bill of lading system has therefore required the elaboration of electronic devices which can offer the functional equivalent of the paper bill of lading.

3 The Electronic Bill of Lading

As the bill of lading is one of the key documents in international trade, there has been great interest in developing an electronic equivalent. Such an "electronic bill of lading" would greatly facilitate international commerce, especially in terms of eliminating the problems generated when shipments arrive at destination before their appertaining bills of lading.

As a consequence of the efficiency of modern transport, cargo shipments (whether by ocean-going vessel or road, rail, air or multi-modal transport) commonly arrive before the relevant bill of lading, which is often sent by mail. One reason for this is that the bill of lading may be negotiated (legally transferred) by endorsement many times before the shipment reaches destination. In order to obtain the release of the goods from the carrier, the ultimate buyer who is not yet in possession of a bill of lading may request a guarantee or letter of indemnity from his bank to convince the carrier to turn the goods over to him against such security despite the absence of a bill of lading. This procedure leads to an unfortunate breakdown in the security offered by the documentary credit system. The electronic bill of lading could therefore provide a solution to this very common problem.

As a result, various electronic bill of lading systems have been proposed over the past few years. To date, none of these has obtained wide acceptance, but the potential of an electronic solution is so great that it can be anticipated that some electronic bill of lading systems will become functional in the near future.

As we have seen in the reference to electronic equivalents in articles A8 and B8 of Incoterms 1990, the first step must be that both parties agree to adopt an electronic replacement for the bill of lading. The Guide to Incoterms (ICC Publication No. 461) includes in an Annex the CMI Rules for Electronic Bills of Lading, which provide a framework for an electronic bill of lading system. While various other systems have been proposed, the issues covered by the CMI Rules are basic to any possible solution. In essence, the carrier must also agree to abide by an electronic system, and must only deliver the goods as electronically instructed by the party having the right to give him delivery instructions. While under a traditional system, only the holder of the paper original bill of lading has the right to give the carrier delivery instructions, under the CMI system only the holder of an electronic "private key" will have this right. Possession of the private key is thus analogous to physical possession of the bill of lading. The private key would take the form of a code known only to one party.

Under the CMI system, when the holder of the private key wishes to transfer his property right to a new holder, he instructs the carrier to this effect and the carrier cancels the old private key and issues a new one to the new holder. In this way, there is only one possible holder of the private key at any given time, just as under the traditional system only one party could be in possession of an original bill of lading (or original set of several bills).

One criticism of the CMI system has been that it makes the carrier the repository of sensitive information and requires shippers and their clients to entrust carriers with the central operative role. An early centralized bill of lading initiative failed for similar reasons. The SEADOCS project, set up by Chase Manhattan bank in the 1980s, installed the bank as the central agent and acceptor of all bills of lading and registrar of all transfers. Theoretically this allowed transfers to take place more quickly and easily, but the project foundered because traders were not content to cede so much power to the bank.

Most recently, the BOLERO electronic bill of lading initiative sponsored by the Commission of the European Communities, seeks to make use of previous experience by using the CMI Rules as a foundation, but with one major difference. Under the BOLERO system, the central register will be held by a trusted third party independent of the shipper, carrier and ultimate buyer.

As a final word, it should be noted that the difficulties posed by the characteristic of negotiability of the electronic bill of lading would not have to be faced if parties could be convinced to use non-negotiable documents (such as sea waybills) which, as we have seen, can be transposed into an electronic context with little difficulty. EDI international trading would be greatly facilitated if traders only used negotiable documents when absolutely necessary. Many traders, however, continue to use bills of lading regardless of convincing arguments for replacing them with less complicated documents such as sea waybills. Moreover, the preference of banks for negotiable documents as forms of security in documentary transactions assures that the traditional bill of lading will continue to be widely used in international trade.

4 Other legal issues raised by EDI practice

Many other legal issues arise in an EDI context. Clearly, the mention of EDI in the Incoterms 1990 does not resolve all the legal issues surrounding EDI use. As a radically new way of doing business, EDI conflicts with legal principles based on the primacy of paper documents. Many national laws require the use of paper documents in particular cases. For example, in the U.S. the Statute of Frauds requires a signed writing for all sales of goods valued over $500. In sea transport, negotiable bills of lading must be represented by signed paper documents. Transfers of real estate often require a great variety of official paper documents. Tax authorities often require that sales be evidenced by paper invoices.

The very concept of "signature" becomes ambiguous when transposed into an electronic context, because EDI is unable to transmit a manual signature in original form. Several schemes, such as the CMI Rules for Electronic Bills of Lading, have proposed versions of an "electronic key" to replace the signature but none of these systems has yet gained broad acceptance.

Another legal issue is the liability of commercial networks to their users. Such network service providers, also known as VANs (Value-Added Network service providers) are third parties which provide services to facilitate data interchange to those parties who agree to communicate via EDI. For the present, VANs have declined to accept such responsibility, which means that a user who suffers economic consequences from an erroneous electronic messages (i.e. a shipment is sent to the wrong party), would not be contractually entitled to legal redress. Even if such a party did institute a law suit, in many cases it is impossible to predict how courts would interpret electronic evidence.

Companies wishing to enter into EDI networks should carefully consider the relevant legal issues, as set out in the ICC Publication No. 517 "The ICC Guide to EDI Interchange Agreements" by Jeffrey Ritter and Amelia Boss. The EDI Interchange Agreement is a contract between two parties wishing to use EDI, which sets out the communications protocols and standards that they will abide by, and in many cases waives any legal defenses based on the insufficiency of electronic evidence.

Various legal bodies around the world are currently engaged in studies and projects aimed at providing a more solid legal foundation for EDI practices. Thus, the United Nations Commission on International Trade Law (UNCITRAL) has been involved in developing a set of standard legal principles to facilitate EDI legal acceptability[1].

5 Why use EDI: the Business Case

When companies are polled they generally list "time savings" and "speed of response," along with "increased order speed" as the most common reasons for adopting EDI. The next most important reasons include "cost savings," "greater accuracy," "better customer relations," "better access to data," and "better control of stocks". Interestingly, only 2% of respondents in one European survey[2] listed "reduction of staff" as a reason for EDI.

Although many people express a fear that advanced technologies such as EDI will lead to widespread unemployment and a situation where "one black box is talking to another black box", in reality firms that increase efficiency with EDI often end up re-assigning their personnel from uninteresting computer-entry jobs to more challenging positions in sales and customer service.

Most companies have initially adopted EDI in their purchasing, order-taking and invoicing departments because of EDI's ability to reduce costs there. Electronically handled, these business tasks are performed faster, with virtually no mistakes, and with a neat, computerized record.

It has been estimated that without EDI up to 70% of all computer output is manually re-keyed in elsewhere, with resultant loss of time and multiplication of costly error. To illustrate the type of business problem solved by EDI, one may observe the case of a U.K. retail chain that prior to adopting EDI had received 30,000 paper invoices a week, employing 19 people just to key them in to its computer system[3]. The inefficiency of these paper-based systems is reflected in estimates showing that up to 10% of the cost of goods stems from the manipulation of paper documents alone. This may also explain why reports of rapid returns on EDI investment are fairly common.

For example, a major American parcel service implemented an EDI system at one of its data processing centres and in eight months was able to reduce paper printouts by 20%[4]. An EDI Coordinator for a major European automobile manufacturer summarized a typical situation in the automobile sector (one of the leading users of EDI because of its need for just-in-time manufacturing): "Right now we are doing about 400,000 EDI transactions a month, and saving about $2 per invoice, with our suppliers saving similar amounts per order. The elimination of re-keying errors has meant fewer disputes and litigation with our suppliers, and they have become much more responsive to our needs[5]."

While the U.S. still leads in market penetration with approximately 60% of the worldwide EDI market[6], Europe is rapidly catching up, thanks in part to the European Community's ambitious TEDIS program (Trade Electronic Data Interchange Systems), and certain Asian countries are moving very quickly into EDI. Singapore, notably, has made a reputation for itself as one of the most innovative and dynamic users of EDI, especially in their port management and customs system.

One of the messages that EDI consultants try to convey is that EDI is more than just a cost-cutting tool. Most importantly, EDI confers strategic and competitive advantages.

While rudimentary forms of EDI have been around for many years (as in computerized airline reservation systems), two recent developments allowed EDI to make a quantum leap forward in terms of business acceptance. First, evolved standards made EDI more reliable, and secondly, a veritable explosion in the variety of EDI services offered by VANs gave users a wide choice of business tools.

6 What are the EDI standards?

Two international EDI standards have gradually achieved predominance: the official North American standard, ANSI ASC X.12 (American National Standards Institute Accredited Standards Committee X.12), and the United Nations' EDIFACT (EDI For Administration, Commerce and Trade), the latter having also been endorsed by the International Standards Organization (ISO). EDI message standards are necessary because of the tremendous diversity of incompatible computer systems in use around the world.

EDIFACT represents an attempt to create a universal structure which allows information elements to pass directly from one computer to another, even if the computer hardware and software are different and incompatible.

EDI standards can be compared to spoken languages, in that they are composed of "messages," "message units" and "syntax" in the same way that a language is composed of words, sentences and grammar. The purpose of an EDI standard is for a trading company to send a document, such as an invoice, to any other trading company in such a fashion that the other company's computer will instantly recognize the document as an invoice, and be able to conduct computer operations on the invoice information (as by incorporating it directly into accounting software). Because of the central importance of the invoice in international trade, the invoice message was one of the very first standards approved by the EDIFACT board[7].

Although EDIFACT continually grows in importance[8], a confusing welter of proprietary or sectoral standards remain, such as ODETTE for the European automotive industry and TRADACOMS for the U.K. retailing industry, but most of the proprietary or industry-specific standards have promised to eventually consolidate with EDIFACT.

For the near future, however, it appears that X12 and EDIFACT will co-exist, with X12 dominant in the North and South America and in some Pacific Rim countries, and EDIFACT dominant in Europe. Some experts are not even convinced that the arrival of a single standard is practicable or desirable[9]. They argue that the desire to standardize EDI at all costs runs contrary to commercial realities. It is in any event likely that several major norms will co-exist. EDIFACT may become the lingua franca for those sectors that are typically international, such as customs and sea transport. In any event, translation software will make it possible to work with several different norms.

Certain experts have also voiced doubts about the possibility and even desirability of obtaining a single universal standard[10]. The fact that each industry sector has a highly specific way of communicating amongst its members renders it arguable that it is feasible to have a single standard for communication both within a single industry and between different industries. These experts argue that in the same way that different dialects are developed by the users of a spoken language, different EDI communities will rely on different standards or different versions of a standard.

7 What EDI standards are used in transport and port management?

Under the EDIFACT standards a set of messages have been developed specifically for the transport area. These are known as the International Forwarding and Transport Message Group (IFTM). The purpose of these messages is to provide a tool for improving service between the customer and the transport company. EDIFACT Customs messages also enable customs declarations to be made electronically from one's office. The Singaporean TradeNet system is one of the most advanced in the world in this area. It is expected that it will eventually be possible for a company to keep track of its merchandise throughout the entire transport process, even while the merchandise is in transport thousands of miles away.

Transport messages have so far been approved for provisional and firm bookings, shipping instructions, contract status (similar to the non-negotiable waybill), and arrival notices. Additional messages will be added after further discussion and testing.

In terms of port community systems there are advanced networks currently in place in diverse ports such as Hamburg, Bremen, Felixstowe, Rotterdam, Marseilles and Singapore. These systems go far towards creating a "paperless" environment with respect to import and export procedures within the port, but international links between ports are still rare. The very strong competition between ports may explain why neighbouring ports are not rapidly connecting to each other. However, distant ports such as Singapore and Antwerp have formed electronic linkages.

8 Who offers EDI services?

Aside from standards development, the other major factor in EDI growth today has been the explosion in services offered by the Value Added Networks. These so-called VANs are generally targeted at specific industries, and provide a complete range of EDI services for their clients, from software and networking to consulting and training.

The variety of services offered is evidenced in the bewildering array of acronyms bandied about at EDI trade shows. Among the best-established networks are ODETTE, for automotive industry suppliers; SWIFT, for global inter-bank transfers; SITA, for international air transport; EDIFICE, for computer suppliers; RINET for reinsurance; FXNET, for foreign exchange; and ALLEGRO for merchandising.

The VANs have on occasion been criticized for practising obscure pricing policies. Clients complain that it is difficult for them to make price comparisons between two VANs because the pricing schemes are so diverse. VANs tend to respond that pricing analyses are possible, but they are often complex and therefore difficult for small companies, because a company must carefully attempt to predict the volume of EDI messages it intends to send. Such predictions are difficult for companies lacking in prior EDI experience.

9 How common is EDI in international trade?

International EDI is still more of a dream than a reality, with some estimates indicating that only 2% of current EDI trading involves cross-border flows. Europe is likely to be the spawning ground for many future international networks, because of expanding intra-Union trade.

Because of the tremendous amount of official red tape and paper documentation required in international trade, this appears to be an area where EDI could provide the greatest benefits. International trade operates on the basis of a continual exchange of information between trading partners and their transporters, insurers, banks, and other parties.

At the present time, these exchanges of information are evidenced by a paper trail that may involve, in a typical international sale, 50 different documents. In the air cargo industry, one shipment can require several different airway bills. Whenever the shipment changes airlines or passes through customs, someone has to sit at a keyboard and type in more data, producing more redundant paper, and often introducing mistakes. It is not surprising that as many as 50% of letters of credit are initially rejected because of errors in the documents, and up to 30% of customs documents also contain errors. Yet all of these different documents are based on the same pieces of information. Ideally, an exporter should only have to type the information into his computer once, and the computer would do the rest. Various commercial networks are seeking to provide this kind of "end-to-end" electronic international commerce, but none has yet advanced beyond the pilot phases.

10 Conclusion: What is the future of EDI?

As a network technology EDI is expected to show continued growth because it still has only penetrated a small fraction of total trading companies. Network technologies are often described by economists as obeying a special principle of growth, known as "positive network externalities," which means that as the network grows it also increases in value. For example, a single telephone is of no use to anyone, but once two telephones are connected they become valuable. With each additional person joining the network, it becomes more valuable for the original users. As the service grows in value it becomes more attractive for non-users, who eventually may find themselves obliged to join if they are not to lose business. This has been the case with the telephone and the fax and explains the explosive growth of these technologies. It is expected to eventually be the case with EDI. Companies which do not have EDI will find themselves locked out of an enormously valuable network.

Notes

1. UNCITRAL has contributed to the preparation of the ICC's "Uniform Rules of conduct for the interchange of trade date by teletransmission" (UNCID Rules) which contain minimum standards of professional care and behaviour for commercial parties engaged in a trade deal involving EDI, cf. ICC Publication No. 452.

2. TEDIS (Trade Electronic Data Interchange Systems) Survey of EDI in all the Member States (Commission of the European Communities 1989) p.15.

3. "Electronic Documentation Offers Greater Efficiency" in International Herald Tribune, March 14, 1990.

4. "Clinging to Paper" in Communications Week International, August 13, 1991.

5. Information provided to the author by Andre Chastel, EDI Manager for Renault Automobiles SA.

6. "Electronic Trade Overview", a lecture given by Norman Barber at a conference on "Worldwide Electronic Commerce", New York, 1994.

7. At present, there are five UN/EDIFACT Boards in operation, viz. the Western European Board, the Eastern European Board, the Pan American Board, the Asian Board, and the Australia/New Zealand EDIFACT Board.

8. It is expected that the UN/EDIFACT Standard will become the leading standard in the world. In a ballot held in Autumn 1992 among the members of ANSI, 76% of the ballots returned approved a motion for the UA X.12 Committee to more to EDIFACT for future message development, both for national and international use, after version 4 of the American National Standard, expected in 1997; "EDIFACTS: The Bulletin of the Western European EDIFACT Board", Issue 14, Autumn 1992, SITPRO Publication, page 1.

9. See "Achieving Global EDI" in Communications Week International, 13 August 1991.

10. "The Design, Adoption and Economic Effects of EDI Standards", Paul David, Stanford University Research Office, April 1991.

Incoterms and UCP 500

JEAN GUEDON

MICHEL-JEAN GAUTHIER

1 Documentary Credits: the 1993 "Uniform customs and practice" (UCP 500)

1.1 Introduction

The "Uniform Customs and Practice for Documentary Credits" (better known as the UCP 500) were published by the ICC in May 1993[1] and have been in force since 1st January 1994. The original version of the rules dates back to 1933 and they have since been regularly updated in order to take account of technological advances on the one hand and of developing trade practices on the other. This present revision is the fifth one[2].

This chapter is divided into four main sections. First, we shall examine the UCP 500, identifying the main differences with the UCP 400, particularly in connection with the rules relating to transport documents. Illustrations of practical problems which may arise under the rules will be given. (A comparative table of the terms used in Incoterms and UCP 400/500 is included in Appendix 1 to this chapter.) The second section of this chapter examines the main purpose of Incoterms 1990 and UCP 500. In the third section, we shall examine the impact of the choice of a particular incoterm upon the documents to be tendered under the letter of credit. The last section refers to new documents referred to in the latest versions of the UCP and Incoterms, and to documents and trade terms no longer referred to therein.

1.2 Main changes relating to documents in UCP 500 as compared with UCP 400

The new UCP 500 text shows a 53% increase in volume from the UCP 400 text. In fact more than a revision, it is a redrafting. In particular, it contains more detail on the various duties, the contents of documents (especially transport documents)[3], the standards for examination of documents, etc.

Although the wording is clearer and the style is better organized (with detailed articles and sub-articles) and more rigorous, it is obvious that all the different parties involved in documentary credits have more provisions to scrutinise.

Among the main changes relating specifically to documents are the following:

(i)   Standards for examination of documents:

Original, copy, full set, signature, issuer, authenticity, clean, probative evidence, incomplete or unclear instructions, discrepancies, payment, etc.

(ii)   Revision of the UCP 400 articles 25 and 26 (Sea transport)

(iii)   Transports: Air, Road, Rail, Inland Waterway, Post, Courier

(iv)   Charterparty bills

(v)   Seawaybill (non-negotiable)

(vi)   Multimodal Transport Document

(vii)   Multimodal Transport Operator

(viii)   Documents Issued by freight forwarders

(ix)   Suppression of the FIATA combined transport bill of lading document

(x)   Insurance (full set of originals, open cover pre-signed...)

(xi)   Where there is no stipulation of the documents to be presented (documents not stipulated)

(xii)   Commercial Invoice (signature not required)

A number of other areas covered by the UCP 500 also have an impact on the tender of documents:

(i)   the obligation to check the apparent authenticity of the credit;

(ii)   the obligation to issue the credit; the issuance of a preliminary advice;

(iii)   negotiation: payment and not only examination of documents;

(iv)   when the draft is drawn on a bank (not on the applicant);

(v)   quantification of the "reasonable time" allowed for the examination of the documents (7 banking days, notification of the decision, etc);

(vi)   statement of all discrepancies;

(vii)   validity (place for presentation, dates for shipment, period of time, expiry date, etc.);

(viii)   liabilities of the banks;

(ix)   issuance referring to a previous credit (this is not desirable);

(x)   amendments to the documentary credit (the credit is irrevocable for the issuing bank but there is no obligation to extend the confirmation);

(xi)   transferable documentary credit.

1.3 Framework of presentation of the rules relating to Documents.

The UCP 500 concerns mainly

- the documents themselves: articles 20 to 38;
- the standards for examination of documents: article 13, together with articles 14 to 19.

In this version of the UCP, although it was not possible to maintain exactly the same structure for all the articles dealing with documents[4], it seems that a real effort for clarification has been made through following, whenever it was possible, a certain standardisation of presentation, i.e.:

- issuers and signers;
- indications that the goods have been collected for carriage;
- place of shipment/destination;
- full set of originals;
- transhipment.

1.4 Evolution in the use of Documentary Credits in relation to Incoterms.

1.4.1 Preliminary remark

Incoterms are not explicitly mentioned in the UCP 500 (except in article 34 relating to the insured value in which CIF and CIP are expressly referred to). This is to be expected because the UCP focuses on payment and on the fact that the seller/buyer relation might vary according to the commercial operation considered. As the contract for the opening of a letter of credit is different and independent from the contract of sale, "delivery" as a legal operation representing the end of the seller's obligations may not need to be mentioned. However, the documents that might be required under Incoterms are featured in a very detailed manner[5] and it will be the selected incoterm which will stipulate which party will have to supply these documents. In that sense, one is entitled to say that they cannot be dissociated from the UCP. The incoterm will be decided upon in the course of the commercial negotiation.

Although there is no direct relation between Incoterms and UCP 500, they are closely related. Neither will prevail over the other but they must absolutely be in compliance with one another.

1.4.2 Evolution

The development of the use of letter of credits in relation to Incoterms may be analyzed from different points of view:

(1) Evolution of the use of letters of credit ;
(2) Evolution of International Trade;
(3) Evolution of Techniques;
(4) Evolution of documentary credits practices in relation to incoterms.

1.4.2.1 Evolution of the use of letter of credit

It might be useful to recall that the letter of credit is only part of a comprehensive whole which is described in the diagram enclosed in Annex 2 to this chapter, "Lay-out of the 4 phases of the International Commercial Operation". That is why one must bear in mind that the existence, terms and consequences of the letter of credit are felt throughout the commercial phase.

Furthermore, the letter of credit is no longer merely restricted to the sale of goods. It is increasingly being used with other different types of sales, e.g. services, studies, surveys, software programmes, turn-key plants, repairs, periodic servicing, maintenance, technical assistance, shows, etc. The developments in these fields are currently taking place very fast. Although some services may not involve the use of transport, other types of services, to a certain extent, will require transportation and, hence, the negotiation of an incoterm:

- a term of payment is frequently linked to the moment of delivery;
- repairs, periodic servicing and maintenance involve the forwarding of spare parts;
- technical assistance frequently includes the use of equipments;
- materials account for more than 50% of the price breakdown of a turn-key plant.

Finally, standby letters of credit (another form included in UCP 500), used either as a payment guarantee but also, more and more, as contract guarantees (tender bonds, performance bonds, advance payment bonds, etc.) lie astride, as under a classical letter of credit, a sale contract which is itself governed by an incoterm.

1.4.2.2 Evolution of International trade

As indicated in the introduction to this chapter, both technological advances and changes in trade practice have necessitated developments in documentary credits and in Incoterms.

Regarding developments in documentary credits, the seller's financial security requirements will correspond more and more to the buyer's quality and service requirements i.e. quality certificate, multimodal transport and incoterms under the "C"- and "D"-groups.

1.4.2.3 Technological Evolution

In all sectors, techniques have changed and evolved rapidly. There is a moment when the combined effort of all these changes is bound to generate a complete mutation instead of distinctive evolutions in parallel. As a matter of fact, these various technical evolutions will influence each other and will require after some time deep changes in working methods.

There are three main fields to be considered:

(i) *Logistics*: for example, supplying and manufacturing under a zero stock policy, container, multimodal, truck, roll-on-roll off, airplane, hubs, integrators, courier and expedited delivery service, etc.

(ii) *Transmission of the information and documents:* for example teletransmission, electronic data interchange (EDI), SWIFT, fax, etc.

(iii) *Administrative work:* for example, export softwares, micro-computers, internal date processing networks, etc.

1.4.2.4 Evolution of documentary credit practices in relation to Incoterms

Any contact with practice will show that trade practice rarely keeps pace with technological advance. Thus some letters of credit, particularly those opened in certain geographical areas, are still based on outdated procedures. Moreover, customs and practices developed in sea transport many centuries ago, as for example FOB, CFR and FAS[6], might effect other incoterms and means of transport.

At the moment although it is possible to open a letter of credit by teletransmission (for example, teletransmission by SWIFT takes 7 minutes between Lima in Peru and Bremen in Germany), this speed, which is normal in the light of today's means of communication, is not exactly quite the same for the whole documentary chain. The improvement of global efficiency is coming up against old habits and practices.

Thus, for example, the voyage across the Mediterranean from Europe to North Africa takes less than 2 days for the vessel to arrive at the African port but the essential document (original of the bill of lading) may take more than 2 weeks to arrive. As it is not possible to keep the boat alongside the quay while waiting for the original of the bill of lading, what happens is that either this document will travel with the goods in the ship's bag on the vessel, or a document other than the bill of lading (i.e. a sea waybill or Multimodal Transport Document) or a different incoterm (FCA, CIP, DDU, etc.) is used. It is now the first solution which still prevails out of habit, conformity or custom.

But what is the value of the bill of lading in these circumstances as a document giving security under a letter of credit? Isn't this a guarantee which in many cases is more an illusion than a reality? At best, would it not be a security which is very difficult to realize in practice?

1.4.3 Examples

To emphasise the above-mentioned theoretical questions, it will be good to give a few practical examples. The following ones are recent and two of them are based on the UCP 500. It must be noted that none of them refers specifically to a particular version of Incoterms. Indeed, the result would be the same, whether they referred to Incoterms 1990 or 1980. In fact, the result would be the same under Incoterms 1953, if not 1936. These examples are an illustration of the fact that old practices remain and create difficult situations for the seller and the buyer.

first example:

- *The facts:* In this case, goods were imported to the European Union from South Korea, payable through a letter of credit governed by the UCP 500, the credit to be irrevocable but not confirmed, available by sight payment. The proforma invoice stipulated the incoterm "FOB South Korea", but with ... an air transport, freight collect, transport insurance of the goods at the buyer's expense and payment against full set of bills of lading.

- *The consequences:* As the terms and conditions of the letter of credit could not be satisfied, the seller could not be paid. It was necessary to modify the terms included in the credit and in that respect to negotiate an amendment. This brought about a substantial waste of time (trebling the duration of the commercial operation) and numerous misunderstandings and suspicions between the seller and the buyer.

- *Why:* Although it was an "air transport" which was used, it was the reference to FOB which prevailed. In this term, the document provided by the seller can only be a sea transport document.

- *What could have been done:* Using an incoterm suited to air transport (FCA, CPT, CIP, DDU), either directly with the air waybill, or if the seller wished to take more precautions by forwarding the goods to a warehousing company based on the European airport which, in turn, would deliver them to the buyer after agreement of the bank which effected payment.

second example:

- *The facts:* In this case, goods were exported from a country of the European Union to Abu Dhabi, payable through a letter of credit governed by the UCP 500, the credit to be irrevocable and confirmed, available by negotiation of a draft at sight (a 5 page letter of advice, opened by mail), with requirements for a lot of documents (no less than 15 different documents among which several are made of several pages) and 3 levels of visas (documents duly certified by a Chamber of Commerce of the country of origin, and also approved by the Joint Arab Chamber of Commerce and legalised by the U.A.E. embassy).

The incoterm is "C&F". One special document must be sent to Abu Dhabi for the insurance.

- *The consequences:* Despite the complexity of the documents, the operation succeeds.

- *Why this complexity:* In this example, the letter of credit requirements are unnecessarily complicated, with fifteen different documents required, each running to several pages. This degree of complexity brings no greater security to the buyer regarding the conformity of the goods with the contract of sale. Rather the reverse: such complexity will inevitably generate unnecessary errors and litigation. This is hardly in keeping with the central purpose of letters of credit, which is to expedite payment as smoothly as possible. Fewer, well-chosen and well-described documents are more likely to assist than needless complexity.

- *What could have been done*: Using a good incoterm, simplifying the terms, conditions and documents, using the SWIFT opening, but on the other hand if the seller wants to be assured of the quality of the goods, demanding a goods inspection certificate (from SGS or similar companies). It is during the commercial negotiation that arrangements must be made. It must be stressed that, in such operations, many documents are asked for by the buyer for the import clearance. Of course, the seller will provide them, and in this case, he could as well take in charge the import customs operations. There are cases of such operations under a DEQ duty paid term.

third example:

- *The facts:* In this case, goods were exported from a country of the European Union to a North African country, payable through a letter of credit governed by the UCP 400, the credit, opened by telex, to be irrevocable and confirmed, available by acceptance of a draft at 90 days, date of CMR. The incoterm is FOT: T is for railway wagon; shipment from a European port to a North African port; and with a CMR (Road transport document) as transport document, which could be presented for the draft acceptance.

- *The consequences:* Such an operation is unfeasible, except if we use a lorry (in order to obtain the CMR), loaded onto a wagon (in order to comply with the FOT incoterm) and the resulting vehicle itself on board a vessel (in order to meet the shipment requirements). This brought about a substantial waste of time and numerous misunderstandings and suspicions between the seller and the buyer.

- *Why*: It is clear that there has been a complete mix-up between the incoterms, documents, means of transportation, etc.. It would have been easier to modify completely the terms and the conditions of the letter of credit by an amendment indicating the right incoterm and the documents required. In fact, we can think that the transport was roll on-roll off. The right term should have been FCA.

• *What could have been done:* Negotiating the text of the letter of credit with its terms (incoterms, documents, means of transportation...), at the same time as the contract of sale.

2 Incoterms1990 and UCP 500

The 1990 version of Incoterms has changed the number of documents, mainly the transport documents, involved in the operations between the seller and the buyer. We can notice the same trend in the new UCP implemented at the beginning of 1994. The two main documents embraced by the ICC were the sea waybill and the Multimodal Transport Document. But documents of other modes of transport have been added, too, both in Incoterms and in the UCP. Thus, we come to a certain harmonization between both sets of rules. This fact is quite natural if we consider the general trend of international trade.

First, there is a development in sea transport of simplified documents such as the "data freight receipt", which can be classified as a sea waybill. Second, the need for a document covering the whole carriage of goods from the point of departure at the seller's premises to the point of arrival at the buyer's premises has brought about the Multimodal Transport Document. The old expression "combined transport" has become obsolete and no more appropriate since, in common parlance, it was often used to indicate the carriage of loaded road vehicles on wagons. Moreover, the rules governing combined transport needed to be renewed.

It must be stressed that the main purpose of the new version of Incoterms was to adapt them to new transport techniques and EDI procedures[7]. The transport techniques had naturally some influence on the new drafting of the UCP, but EDI did not play such a determining role in the redrafting of the UCP. The main people involved, i.e. bankers, are very cautious on the subject. In fact, UCP 500 does not refer directly to EDI but does make provision for cases where parties are using it as their means of communication[8].

Documents have always been considered as important in Incoterms and have been particularly developed in the 1990 version.

Documents are also the basis of documentary credits. Thus it can be said that Incoterms and the UCP are complementary, though separate and independent sets of rules. Incoterms are a stipulation of the contract of sale. The letter of credit is not included in this contract but is a special agreement, and, though requested by the seller, it is concluded between the buyer and his banker.

As stressed in article 3 of the UCP[9], the two contracts are independent. But the banker wants a kind of delivery in which there is a minimum of risks for him. Since the main purpose of Incoterms is to give a clear definition of delivery, and delivery signifies the end of the seller's obligations, they are quite important for the banker, because he has to pay the seller. The best conditions are when the seller has fulfilled his obligations, detains the transport document evidencing that the goods have been loaded on board or shipped, and does not bear any more risks. That is the reason why the "C"-terms are preferred by the bankers. A banker will not, as a general rule, pay a seller who has not yet fulfilled all his obligations and bears risks, e.g. under a "D"-term (except, in some cases, DAF) or a seller who cannot tender a transport document evidencing that the goods have been loaded on board or shipped, i.e. under "E"- and "F"-terms (except in the cases when the seller contracts for carriage.)

It must also be underlined that, while the UCP 500 do not mention Incoterms, the Introduction to the text of Incoterms and the Guide to Incoterms develop some guidelines about documentary credits. In the Guide, comments under article B8 of all incoterms – except EXW – refer to letters of credit, which means that, from the point of view of Incoterms, all terms can be used in connection with a documentary operation, although clearly the problems created by documents for banker and traders are quite different.

3 Use of incoterms in documents tendered under letters of credit

A letter of credit always requires at least three documents: a commercial invoice, a transport document and evidence of insurance cover. The main document is the transport document (article A8 of Incoterms). It indicates that the goods exist, that they are under the responsibility of a carrier and that this carrier undertakes to carry them to a named destination. It is common practice to name the issuing bank as consignee, though less common where the document is a bill of lading. It is a sort of guarantee for this bank.

The certificate of insurance (article A3 of CIF and CIP) is the necessary complement to the transport document strengthening the security both of the banker as well as that of the party bearing the risk under the contract of sale. It is absolutely necessary for the beneficiary, i.e. the seller, to obtain these two documents. Thus, Incoterms are important because they dictate who has to procure these documents.

This is also true of other documents. Quite often a letter of credit requires not just the three above-mentioned documents, but also others such as certificates, authorizations, etc.. Articles A2 and B2, A10 and B10 of all incoterms indicate who will provide such documents. This may determine the choice of the incoterm.

As aforesaid, where the EXW term is used, a letter of credit does not enter into consideration. The only obligation of the seller is to put the goods at the disposal of the buyer at his own premises. He is not concerned with the subsequent operations and could not procure the necessary documents.

The "F"-terms are not easy to use with letters of credit but, in certain circumstances, they can be used. In the case of FCA or FOB, the seller can contract for carriage at the buyer's cost and risk, if both parties so agree, and he will obtain a transport document, but, in FCA, it will be, for a sea carriage, a "received for shipment" bill of lading and it will be necessary to add later the mention "on board", which will take some time. As for the FAS term, the document will be "received for shipment", and it cannot be seen how the seller could get a bill of lading since the Hague Rules indicates that this document must be given by the carrier to the shipper, i.e. the person who contracts with him, in this case, the buyer. In the text of this incoterm, nothing indicates that the seller could conclude the contract of carriage with the agreement of the buyer. Furthermore, this document will commonly be issued by a person who is not a carrier and will deliver a dock receipt, a forwarding agent's certificate of receipt (FCR), etc., or, if the goods have been received by a carrier, perhaps the carrier will issue a "received for shipment" bill of lading, which is a proof of delivery, but no more than that.

The insurance in an "F"-term is normally covered by the buyer who bears the risks of the main transport. He can send the certificate to the seller, though, practically, this is not easy. Nevertheless, it is practised by buyers who have the obligation to insure the goods in their own country and buy FOB. Another solution is that the seller takes care of the insurance for the buyer's account. Another one is that the seller has an "open policy" which automatically insures all the goods he is sending. Solutions do need to be found because there are many countries that lack strong currency, and buy FOB to carry on their own ships and oblige their buyers to take the insurance in their own country. Moreover, the sale is made under a documentary credit and clear documentary instructions are therefore necessary.

One fact to notice is that in some countries such as Australia and New Zealand, a commercial term is commonly used which is not an incoterm, namely the so-called "C+I". It can be analyzed as a FCA or FOB "plus insurance". Such a term could be used, but only after having been converted into a regular incoterm such as FCA or FOB. Of course, the specifications of the insurance cover should be given, and the seller should contract for carriage as an additional service to his main obligation of delivery.

The "C"-terms, mainly CIF and CIP, are the most commonly used in conjunction with letters of credit. The seller has the documents and when he hands over these documents to the bank for payment and delivers conforming goods to the carrier, he has fulfilled his obligation to deliver. In CFR and CPT, insurance should normally be taken by the buyer since he bears the risks of the main carriage. It is possible to find a solution like that adopted for the "F"-terms. In some countries, buyers are automatically insured for all their imports by the national insurance company. The seller contacts this company, sends a reference given to him by the buyer at the time of the contract and receives the certificate of insurance.

It must be added that the "C"-terms are widely used by sellers for whom the letter of credit is not only a guarantee of payment but also a means to be paid as soon as the goods are loaded on a ship, e.g. in many countries of Central and South America, or South East Asia.

The "D"-terms are not favoured by bankers, because the payment will take place only when the seller will have fulfilled his obligation of delivery, generally in another country. It must be underlined that for several years the letter of credit was associated with a "C"-term. Bankers are not yet accustomed to the "D"-terms. Their development has been important only in the past few years. For some of these bankers, a standby letter of credit will be more useful and less expensive.

However, some "D"-terms are used with letters of credit. As an example, trade is developing between EC and Central and Eastern Europe countries. It is an old practice of those countries to use the DAF, for road as well as rail transport. Needless to say, the goods are generally sold under letters of credit. The same fact could occur in a rail carriage between Spain and another European country since the tracks are not the same and a shifting of the goods is necessary at the Franco-Spanish border, but there is little use of letters of credit in Spain or Portugal. In another field, it is possible that the DES be used with letters of credit.

However, as noticed in the Introduction of Incoterms as well as in the Guide[10], there is a general trend of development of the "D"-terms. There is also a development of bankruptcies in many countries and a need for security of payment, i.e. letters of credit. Both facts should lead to an increase of letters of credit used in conjunction with a "D"-term. Furthermore, whether it is a classic letter of credit or a standby letter of credit does not matter very much since both of them are ruled by UCP 500.

Those are only general rules and their application can depend upon many factors such as the countries, common practice, and the relations between bankers and customers, etc. In fact, the use of the right incoterm with a letter of credit will depend upon the circumstances. For some sellers, letters of credit are a guarantee of payment; for others, it is a means to get paid shortly after the goods have been shipped. For the first ones, the standby letter of credit connected with a "D"-term will be sufficient; for the latter ones, it is advisable to use a "C"-term with the letter of credit. The Guide to

Incoterms explains that all of them, except the EXW, can be used in connection with letters of credit.

A last point must be underlined. In the Guide to Incoterms, comments under article B8 of all incoterms, except EXW, specify that the buyer must accept the transport document if it conforms with the contract and the stipulations of article A8 and if he rejects the document by instructions not to pay the seller under a letter of credit, he commits a breach of contract.

4 New documents

As has already been said, there are more documents mentioned in Incoterms 1990 and in the UCP 500 than in the previous versions, which seemed to consider only sea carriage or combined transport. Other documents were referred to under the general term of transport document. It seems quite normal to detail the names of the documents attached to the other modes of transport. Furthermore, these names are generally those that are given by the international conventions that regulate rail, road and air transports.

In 1980, an International Convention for Multimodal Transport was signed, but it will take some time before it is applied on a world scale. Nevertheless, rules for a Multimodal Transport Document were drafted by UNCTAD – ICC and are now effective. It must be noticed that this document can be negotiable.

The FIATA bill of lading has been omitted in the last version of UCP, there being no particular reason for preferring this document to other similar ones used by other organisations and shipping companies. In the meantime, though, FIATA have drafted a new document in accordance with the UNCTAD-ICC Rules and in accordance with article 30 of the UCP 500, which now allows the tender of freight-forwarder documents in stipulated circumstances.

The "Uniform Rules for Sea Waybills" were drafted by the CMI and are included in the Appendix to the Guide to Incoterms. In fact, the **sea waybill** is a document similar to any transport document for modes of transport other than sea.

Another document making its first appearance in the UCP 500 is the **charterparty bill of lading**. Charterparties are included in Incoterms 1990, too, but from a different angle. There are specific charterparty terms that are often mixed up with incoterms and that may lead to confusion. However, it is indicated in the text of CFR and CIF that, if the transport document refers to a charterparty, the seller must provide a copy of the latter document.

For the UCP, if the charterparty contract is required by the letter of credit, the banks do not have to examine it. Indeed, the charterparty contract is not simply a contract for the carriage of goods and consequently the charterparty is not a transport document. In fact, it often occurs that for goods on chartered vessels, bills of lading contain no reference to the charterparty, because the seller, who is generally the charterer, does not wish to tender the charterparty. He will only give the buyer the necessary information about discharging operations.

In fact, in Incoterms, the main element related to charterparties is the manner in which a charterparty term such as FIO (Free In and Out) will be associated to the incoterm, i.e. the necessary addition to this incoterm in order to specify the operations of loading or discharging. As regards the document, there is no difference between the charterparty bill of lading and a regular shipping line bill of lading.

In the UCP 500, one of the main elements of the bill of lading is the way it should be drafted as this could give rise to a lot of problems. The previous UCP 400 required transport documents referring to a charterparty to be rejected. Consequently, where goods were carried on a chartered vessel, bills of lading frequently failed to make any mention of a charterparty. At times, it was possible to infer from certain terms in the bill of lading that there was indeed a charterparty, but it was difficult to discover whether the seller had performed all the obligations connected with delivery, e.g. stowage and trimming after the goods were loaded on board. Banks were thus in some difficulty in deciding whether or not to pay.

Thus, for example, not so long ago under the UCP 400, a banker read on a bill of lading "C & F, freight prepaid, free out", with another addition "discharging at port of destination including work in the ship's holds to be on the buyer's account." The banker thought that, if there was work in the holds on arrival, there could be some work too after delivery at the port of departure, at the seller's charge, which was not allowed by the letter of credit. He was not to know that the goods, chemicals in bulk, are loaded with a hose, which does not bring any extra charge for the seller, but that unloading is performed by means of grabs and in the end by scraping and shovelling the cargo which was out of reach for grabbing. In fact, "CFR" on the commercial invoice and "freight prepaid" on the bill of lading would have been sufficient: the other additions were mere instructions for the carrier and the buyer.

A last point must be noted. The bill of lading should be completed in the same terms as the charterparty. As an example, if the charterparty mentions as the port of destination "a French port in the range Bordeaux-Dunkirk" and the bill of lading only mentions "a French port", the buyer who is entitled to determine the port of destination might decide to send the goods to a French Mediterranean port according to the bill of lading and the carrier can refuse according to the charterparty. Of course, in this example, there has been a mistake in the drafting of the bill of lading, the responsibility for which falls on the seller-charterer who should have noticed the mistake when receiving the document. The consequences may be serious for the buyer.

Conclusion

Many letters of credit present discrepancies (more than 50% as mentioned in the preface to the UCP 500). But in most cases these discrepancies concern transport documents, and the cause of the problems is frequently that incoterms and documents are not well considered and chosen, leading to discrepancies between the two, as we saw in the third example. The choice of incoterms and documents evidencing delivery needs to be the subject of careful negotiations.

Studies carried out in France by the Centre de Techniques Internationales – CTI – have shown that a financial potential accounting for a minimum of 8 to 12% of the selling price exists in a well negotiated and performed contract of sale.

The latest version of the UCP contains a good number of changes bringing the ICC's rules on documentary credits into line with the latest 1990 version of Incoterms, taking into account both new developments in the transport industry and new technological applications. As explained in this Chapter, there are close links between Incoterms and documentary credits. Although documents form only part of the subject-matter of Incoterms, the rules are important because they make clear whose duty it is to procure which document. In the UCP, which make no specific reference to Incoterms, documents receive much more detailed attention than they do in Incoterms 1990. Moreover, the banking community is familiar with Incoterms and can appreciate which terms are most appropriate for their purposes, i.e. which terms offer them a minimum of risks. However, the fact that both Incoterms and the UCP 500 deal adequately with the documents to be tendered for payment does not relieve the parties to the sale contract from their responsibility to safeguard their own interests through the appropriate negotiation of both the sale contract and the letter of credit. It is not enough for the rules regulating the both contracts to tally: if losses are to be avoided, the contracts themselves must match.

Annex 1

Comparative table of the terms used in Incoterms and UCP 400/500

INCOTERMS 1980

Commercial invoice
Transport document
Bill of lading
Sea waybill

Charterparty
Policy of marine Insurance
Transport insurance policy
Evidence of insurance cover

UCP 400

Commercial invoice
Transport document
Bill of lading
Combined transport bill of lading
      FIATA combined transport
      bill of lading
      Combined transport
      document

Charterparty
Insurance document
Cover note

INCOTERMS 1990

Commercial Invoice
Transport document
Bill of lading
Sea waybill
Inland waterway document
Charterparty

Air waybill
Railway consignment note
Road consignment note
Multimodal Transport Document
Delivery order
Insurance policy
Evidence of insurance cover

UCP 500

Commercial Invoice
Transport document
Bill of lading
Sea waybill
Inland waterway transport document
Charterparty
Charterparty bill of lading
Air transport document
Rail transport document
Road transport document
Multimodal Transport Document

Insurance document
Cover note

Annex 2

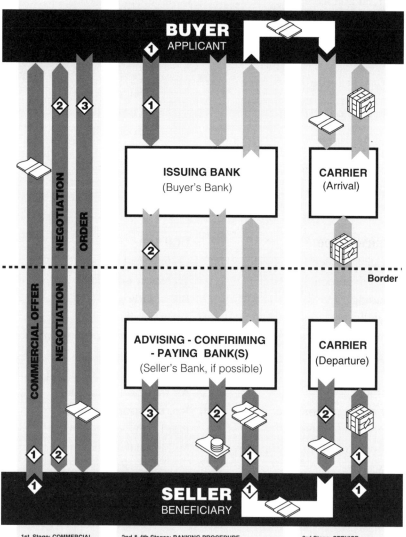

COMPREHENSIVE DIAGRAM of an INTERNATIONAL COMMERCIAL OPERATION

BUYER
APPLICANT

ISSUING BANK
(Buyer's Bank)

CARRIER
(Arrival)

Border

ADVISING - CONFIRIMING - PAYING BANK(S)
(Seller's Bank, if possible)

CARRIER
(Departure)

COMMERCIAL OFFER

NEGOTIATION

ORDER

SELLER
BENEFICIARY

1st Stage: COMMERCIAL
DOCUMENTARY Chain:
COMMERCIAL
■ Commercial Offer
■ Negotiation
■ Order

2nd & 4th Stages: BANKING PROCEDURE
DOCUMENTARY Chain:
CHECKING PROCEDURE and PAYMENT
■ 2nd Stage: Setting up of the "Checking Procedure and Payment" Circuit
■ 4th Stage: Checking Procedure and Payment

3rd Stage: SERVICE
DOCUMENTARY Chain:
SERVICE and LOGISTICS
■ Service Fulfilment and Issurance of the Relevant Documents

Notes

1   ICC Publication No. 500

2   Two complementary Guides edited by Charles del Busto, Chairman of the ICC Commission on Banking Technique and Practice, were published at the same time in 1993:

    (i) UCP 500 and 400 compared (an article-by-article detailed analysis), ICC Publication No.511;

    (ii) Standard Documentary Credit Forms for the UCP 500, ICC Publication No 516.

3   The Guide, "Standard Documentary Credit Forms for the UCP 500" (ICC Publication no. 516) features a documentary credit application form showing a chart with the possible incoterms and the list of the main documents which may be required, with the transport documents given pride of place.

4   This was not feasible since there are documents as different as the bill of lading, the sea waybill, the air transport document, courier and post receipts, the insurance document, the attestation certificate of weight, etc.

5   cf. part 1.2 above-mentioned.

6   These three acronyms date back to more than one and a half centuries ago.

7   cf. Introduction to Incoterms, op. cit., p.6, para.3-4.

8   Under article 20(b) UCP it seems that tender of an electronic bill of lading would be good tender unless explicitly excluded by contract. Note also the reference to "any signature or authentication" in articles 23-30 UCP.

9   "(a) Credits, by their nature, are separate transactions from the sales or other contract(s) on which they may be based and banks are in no way concerned with or bound by such contract(s), even if any reference whatsoever to such contract(s) is included in the Credit. Consequently, the undertaking of a bank to pay, accept and pay Draft(s) or negotiate and/or to fulfil any other obligation under the Credit, is not subject to claims or defences by the Applicant resulting from his relationships with the Issuing Bank or the Beneficiary."

    (b) A Beneficiary can in no case avail himself of the contractual relationships existing between the banks or between the Applicant and the Issuing Bank."

10   op. cit., p.8 and 21.

Incoterms and Insurance

KLAUS B. WINKLER

1 Cover of insurance policy

For eleven of thirteen incoterms, article A3(b) of Incoterms 1990 stipulates no obligation for the seller as concerns the contract of insurance. Article B3 does not expressly release the buyer of the obligation to take out insurance although it must be clear that just as the buyer is not, in these eleven terms, obliged to conclude a contract of carriage, he is likewise not bound to obtain insurance cover. However, it would be wrong to conclude that purchasing insurance cover was totally unnecessary. The intention rather is to let the seller and buyer decide at their discretion about insurance and its extent.

1.1 Scope of cover to be agreed

1.1.1 Conditions

Only CIF and CIP stipulate in article A3(b) that "the seller must obtain ... cargo insurance as agreed in the contract."

What scope of cover should the seller or buyer agree in the contract? This is a question that has to be answered irrespective of which of the thirteen incoterms is agreed. The insurance needed should always be precisely indicated, and therefore mere reference to a "maximum" insurance should not be made. The following wording is recommended:

Model for contract and letter of credit

> Insurance cover at (clearly identified) conditions
>
> from_____ (place of commencement of insurance)
> to _____ (place of termination of insurance)
>
> plus:
>
>   WAR, SRCC
> _____ days storage at insured option
> _____ % anticipated profit
> _____ (if percentage higher or lower than 10% is desired)
> _____ (named) currency (if not the currency of the contract)
> _____ (other particularities)

The scope of cover is to be chosen with account taken of the type of cargo involved and the transport route used. In most cases, the optimum cover is one "against all risks". It covers all risks of loss or damage which may result from perils to which the goods are exposed during the insurance period. Exclusions are listed in the conditions. The most common terms used are the Institute Cargo Clauses (A) issued by the British market. Comparable forms of cover under other insurance conditions are found in most countries.

It is common for those sellers who have to insure numerous shipments to agree an "open cover" with an insurer enjoying their trust. The sellers are aware of the typical properties of the cargo they ship, and insurance cover is tailored to answer their requirements. Then the clause "insurance under open cover no. .... of company .... (named seller)" may be integrated in the contract or letter of credit.

1.1.2 Why do CIF and CIP not require "all risks" cover?

A question often asked is why CIF and CIP only provide minimum insurance and make any improved insurance protection subject to special agreement. Various reasons can be suggested:

a) "All risks" cover is simply not customary for quite a variety of cargo, e.g. sand, gravel, broken rock, asphalt, oil, refrigerated and frozen goods, live animals, valuables and all goods transported unpacked or in bulk such as ore, scrap metal, coal, chemicals, fertilisers, wooden logs, cereals.

b) "All risks" cover also insures the risks of theft, pilferage and robbery. It would be unreasonable if CIF and CIP terms imposed a general obligation on the seller to insure these risks. It is even imaginable that the seller might be unable to obtain any insurance protection against these risks as crime rates are on the increase throughout the world. This is especially true for those goods whose exposure to theft is above average. The following is a useful list of goods running a higher than average exposure to theft.

Goods with high exposure to theft

tires	liquor
clothing	sports articles
cosmetics	wallpaper
furniture	textile products

food	entertainment electronics
leather goods	valuables
furs	wine
personal computers	tools
pharmaceuticals	cigarettes

In some countries, the crime risk is so high that it is only insured if the seller and buyer take special loss-preventing measures with the assistance of a qualified marine insurer. If the contract partners neither intend to take loss-preventive measures against criminal action nor are willing to pay a higher premium to cover their increased risk, the only alternative is to exclude criminal risks in the insurance cover. That is why on-carriage of goods exported nowadays remains uninsured in some countries as cover ends upon discharge of the goods in the port of destination (airport or sea port).

c)   Cargo insurance is a product whose optimal design requires consultancy and risk assessment by the underwriter. If the seller and buyer fail to make any agreement concerning insurance, the information which articles A10 and B10 define will also not be available. In this case, only a minimum cover can be generally obtained.

d)   "All risks" is the most comprehensive cargo coverage that can be purchased. However, it should be borne in mind that all incoterms only define minimum obligations. That applies to insurance cover as well.

1.2   Failing express agreement

1.2.1   Seller has to procure minimum insurance

Applicable minimum cover provided by the Institute of London Underwriters is governed by the Institute Cargo Clauses (C) 1.1.82. They offer protection in the event of named risks, such as fire, explosion, vessel being stranded, grounded or capsized, collision. Moreover, these conditions provide for the payment of general average contributions. The above-mentioned list of examples shows that this cover provides insurance predominantly against total loss and total damage due to specified risks, but it is not a comprehensive all risks cover. There is no cover for damage through breakage in the event of transhipment of goods or loss through theft, pilferage or robbery.

However, the seller is not obliged to take out insurance cover on the basis of these English original conditions. He may choose any other national conditions, e.g. the minimum cover customary at his place of business. Any other insurance cover, however, must be commercially equivalent, in terms of the risks covered, exclusions, claims and duration, to the English cover described in the wording of CIF and CIP. While the cover taken out may provide better protection than the Institute Cargo Clauses (C), the insurance cover obtained must never be less comprehensive than it.

1.2.2 Minimum insurance covers the price plus 10% (i.e. 110%)

CIF and CIP, at article A3(b) specify the minimum insurance cover to include the contract price plus 10%. The purpose of this is to cover the value of the goods at destination. Therefore, the additional 10% represents a profit to third parties.

The idea of an additional 10% goes back to 1906 and the English Marine Insurance Act of that year. The purpose is to cover the average profit which buyers expect from the sale. In fact, this excess insurance is a general custom in certain trades and countries, and was incorporated in the very first edition of Incoterms in 1936. In the cocoa trade, for example, the custom is to cover the invoice price plus 12.5%. In France, international sales contracts are sometimes insured for up to 20% over the invoice value (though this is only the case for contracts involving international transport). However, there is nothing in Incoterms 1990 that prevents the parties from agreeing coverage higher or lower than 110%, provided that both parties to the contract of sale make an express agreement to that effect. It has to be pointed out, however, that the assured will only receive an indemnity for the profit share exceeding 10% if he is able to prove this higher profit.

2   Insurable interest

An "interest" is the relationship that exists between a person and a specific good. Thus the insurable interest is not the good itself but the relationship which the assured has with the good. If a good is lost or damaged only that person will sustain a loss whose relation to the good has deteriorated. In cargo insurance that person generally is the one who had to bear the risk of the good at the time of occurrence of the event insured against.

Articles A5 and B5 of Incoterms 1990 determine the respective legs of a transport for which either the seller or the buyer has to bear the risk of the goods. Only if EXW, DDU or DDP are agreed, will the assured bear the risk of loss of the goods from the place of commencement of transit to the place of destination. All other incoterms provide for a transfer of risk from seller to buyer at some instant during transportation. When loss or damage occurs, the insurer will examine in which phase of the transport the event causing loss occurred and whether an insurable interest of the claimant existed at the time of the occurrence. Without insurable interest there will be no obligation on the part of the insurer to indemnify.

Thus, consider an FOB buyer who procures insurance covering the risks of the voyage. If loss or damage occurs during the pre-carriage to the port of shipment, the buyer's insurer will not indemnify for the damage, as the buyer did not bear the risk of loss of the goods at the time of the occurrence. Only the seller's insurer, if any, would be obliged to indemnify for the loss or damage.

If CIF or CIP is agreed, the seller is therefore obliged to "provide the buyer with the insurance policy or other evidence of insurance cover".

3 Cover of risks from warehouse to warehouse

3.1 Duration

The duration of the insurance cover is determined by the printed conditions for cargo insurance. Cover is provided from the place of commencement of insurance to the place of termination of insurance. In the Institute Cargo Clauses (A) and (C) the duration is determined by the transit clause which is identical in cargo clauses (A) and (C) and which is set out in Annex 1 to this chapter. Storage at the assured's option is excluded in the transit clause. Other national conditions contain similar provisions some of which allow storage at the assured's option for a specified number of days.

An insurance policy or insurance certificate describes an individual insured voyage. It names the place of commencement of insurance, the place of termination of insurance for the respective voyage and also the port of shipment and port of discharge. Only the voyage named in the policy or certificate will be covered for the assured. However, it is possible to extend the cover beyond the expiry determined by Incoterms. Such extensions are very common when CIF is agreed, as this term only applies to the port-to-port carriage.

3.2 From warehouse to warehouse covered with an insurer

One of the parties should preferably insure the complete transport (from warehouse to warehouse) with one insurer. If separate insurances are taken out for the various legs of a journey and loss or damage is ascertained by the consignee only after arrival of the goods, it is often impossible to prove when and where the loss or damage occurred and which of the various insurers has to indemnify.

3.3 Risk gap in EXW

The only "collection clause" found in Incoterms 1990 is EXW. The seller need not worry about the transport of goods. His obligation is to have the goods ready for collection at a specific time and place. It is common for the seller's premises to be agreed as the place of collection. From the collection onwards the buyer will have to bear the risk of the goods. As cover under the cargo insurance does not start before commencement of the transport, there is a risk gap to the buyer's disadvantage.

In some countries, e.g. Germany, the buyer's fire policy may cover this period. In the event of loss or damage the fire insurer will check whether EXW pre-storage was duly considered in the sum insured. If the sum insured is not sufficient, deduction for under-insurance will be made. In other countries, e.g. Great Britain, the buyer's fire insurance does not provide cover for EXW pre-storage, unless this has been specially agreed. The following alternatives are open to the buyer:

a)   EXW should only be agreed when the buyer collects his goods – perhaps with his own trucks – as soon as they are made available. If this is not possible another incoterm should be agreed, e.g. FCA.

b)   Any difference in conditions to the seller's fire policy may be covered under a marine insurance. Combined, these two policies will cover any loss or damage to the cargo.

c)   If the seller does not have a fire policy, the storage risk may be covered under a marine insurance which will then indemnify against the individual risks customarily insured under a fire policy, such as fire, explosion, lightening, impact or crash of aircraft or their parts or cargo.

Both the marine insurer and fire insurer require information about the structural condition and security of the warehouse before issuing cover notes for b) or c) above. As underwriting results are negative worldwide, they are unable to make any uninformed capacity available.

4   Compulsory national insurance in certain countries

Free competition of insurers guarantees that cover is routed to that market which offers optimum cover and service at most reasonable cost. This can only be achieved if seller and buyer are free to decide:

• who purchases insurance cover,
• with which insurer to place the risk.

61 countries deny exporters and importers this freedom. By doing so, governments and authorities of the countries concerned have two targets in mind:

a) **Promotion of national insurance industry**

The idea is understandable when the local insurance sector is too small to be fully competitive. The list of countries stipulating national insurance is headed by a number of developing countries; it also includes some nations, however, which in other respects are economically competitive.

Some countries introduced the obligation to insure locally in the 1940s and 1950s. After 50 years their insurance industries still have not reached a state of competitiveness. And how should they, when they face no international competition?

b) **Saving foreign exchange costs for insurance premiums**

This argumentation tends to forget that claims will be payable in the currency of the sum insured, i.e. in foreign exchange. Lack of foreign exchange results in claims sometimes not being settled at all or only after receipt of reinsurance funds, or in settlement being made in local currency which may not be freely transferable.

The economies of these countries sustain substantial prejudice when goods are destroyed or damaged. Lost imported goods frequently can only be purchased abroad against foreign currency. The sales price for exported goods is to be realised in foreign currency.

National insurance industries develop more favourably when they begin by insuring risks that are commensurate with their financial efficiency. This can also be achieved by accepting shares of insurance contracts. If a policy is led by an experienced foreign insurer with international experience, even a smaller insurer will have a chance to accumulate know-how of its own from this cooperation and thus to become gradually competitive in every respect.

A list of countries with compulsory national insurance is given in Annex 2 to this chapter. The International Union of Marine Insurance (IUMI)/Freedom of Insurance Committee (Circular April 1993, page 2) made the following comments about this list:

"Restrictive measures are described from the view point of the countries listed.

"It is clear that restrictive measures may take a more subtle form than shown below. Furthermore, besides restrictive legal measures, there are hindrances in some countries to the freedom of transport insurance with no legal grounds. In some cases, it appears that the restrictive regulations exist but are not actually applied. However, a listing can still be the case.

"It should also be mentioned that in practice freedom of insurance may not exist in some countries where there are state monopolies of insurance and/or government-controlled trading agencies.

Such situations are not reflected in the list. This list is by no means exhaustive."

Annex 1

Institute Cargo Clauses (A) and (C), Article 8, provide as follows:

Duration

8.1 This insurance attaches from the time the goods leave the warehouse or place of storage at the place named herein for the commencement of the transit, continues during the ordinary course of transit and terminates either

8.1.1 on delivery to the Consignees' or other final warehouse or place of storage at the destination named herein.

8.1.2 on delivery to any other warehouse of place of storage, whether prior to or at the destination named herein, which the Assured elect to use either

8.1.2.1 for storage other than in the ordinary course of transit or

8.1.2.2 for allocation or distribution.

or

8.1.3 on the expiry of 60 days after completion of discharge overside of the goods hereby insured from the overseas vessel at the final port of discharge, whichever shall first occur.

8.2 If, after discharge overside from the overseas vessel at the final port of discharge, but prior to termination of this insurance, the goods are to beforwarded to a designation other than that to which they are insured hereunder, this insurance, whilst remaining subject of termination as provided for above, shall not extend beyond the commencement of transit to such other destination.

8.3 This insurance shall remain in force (subject to termination as provided for above and to the provisions of Clause 9 below) during delay beyond the control of the Assured, any deviation, forced discharge, reshipment or transhipment and during any variation of the adventure arising from the exercise of a liberty granted to shipowners or charterers under the contract of affreightment.

Annex 2

Countries with compulsory national insurance

(1) = Forbidden for the seller to insure exports abroad
(2) = Forbidden for the buyer to insure imports abroad
(3) = Forbidden for the seller to export FOB
(4) = Forbidden for the buyer to import CIF
(5) = Special taxes, extra charges
(6) = Currency restrictions

Algeria	**(2) (4)**	Korea, North	**(2)**
Angola	**(2) (4)**	Libya	**(2) (4)**
Argentina	**(1) (2)**	Malaysia	**(5)**
Austria	**(5)**	Mali	**(2) (4)**
Bangladesh	**(1) (2)**	Mauritania	**(2) (4) (6)**
Barbados	**(2) (5)**	Mexico	**(1) (2)**
Benin	**(2)**	Morocco	**(2)**
Bolivia	**(1) (2)**	Nicaragua	**(2) (4)**
Brazil	**(2)**	Niger	**(2) (6)**
Burundi	**(1) (2)**	Nigeria	**(2) (4)**
Cameroon	**(2) (4)**	Oman	**(2) (4)**
Cape Verde	**(1) (2)**	Pakistan	**(2) (4)**
Central African R.	**(2) (4) (6)**	Panama	**(2) (4)**
Chad	**(2) (4)**	Portugal	**(1) (2)**
Colombia	**(2) (4) (6)**	Rwanda	**(1) (2) (6)**
Congo	**(2) (4)**	Senegal	**(1) (2) (3) (4)**
Cuba	**(3) (4)**	Seychelles	**(1) (2) (6)**
Dominican Rep.	**(2)**	Sierra Leone	**(2)**
Ecuador	**(2)**	Somalia	**(2) (4) (5) (6)**
Ethiopia	**(2)**	Sudan	**(2)**
Gabon	**(2) (3) (4) (6)**	Syria	**(2)**
Ghana	**(1) (2) (3) (4)**	Tanzania	**(2) (4)**
Guinea	**(2) (4)**	Togo	**(2) (5)**
Haiti	**(1) (2) (3) (4)**	Tunisia	**(2) (4)**
Indonesia	**(1) (2)**	Uganda	**(2)**
Iran	**(2) (4)**	Upper Volta/	
Iraq	**(2) (4)**	Burkina Faso	**(2) (4)**
Italy	**(1) (2) (5)**	Venezuela	**(2)**
Ivory Coast	**(2) (4) (6)**	Yemen	**(1) (2)**
Jordan	**(2) (4) (6)**	Zaire	**(1) (2) (6)**
Kenya	**(2) (6)**	Zambia	**(4)**

Reference:

International Union of Marine Insurance (IUMI). Freedom of Insurance Committee, Circular April 1994, pages 3-9.

Incoterms and the Single Market

RAYMOND BATTERSBY

Background

The establishment of the Single Market on 1 January 1993 introduced radical changes to the way that business is conducted between EC trading partners within the European Union, which since the 1st January 1995 was expanded to include Austria, Finland and Sweden. The disappearance of internal frontiers for intra-Community trade has had the effect of creating an internal enlarged domestic market of some 340 million customers. The question asked by traders is what role do Incoterms play in this environment linked to developments elsewhere, e.g. NAFTA, particularly given the requirement under articles A2 and B2 of Incoterms 1990[1] which cover all customs and official clearance formalities and their link as appropriate to articles A6 and B6?

This is very relevant as one of the most important features of the Single Market was the abolition of a host of controls traditionally associated with customs formalities at the frontiers. This has led to the free movement of goods between EC Member States without any official intervention, other than spot checks carried out by customs for anti-smuggling purposes.

On a wider canvas, the abolition of internal frontiers within the EC has undoubtedly provided opportunities for improved business performance. Speedier movements through ports and airports as a result of no longer having to complete customs clearance formalities, have significantly reduced delivery times. Transport costs have also been drastically lowered as sellers and buyers no longer have to bear the costs of raising customs documentation for intra-Community movements.

Single market changes

The most noticeable change in official requirements is that the abolition of the Single Administrative Document (SAD) with regards to trade between Member States[2] has released EC traders from the obligations of completing customs declarations at internal frontiers.

However, national administrations still require information for revenue and statistical purposes. This was, of course, previously captured by the SAD on a transaction basis. An alternative system had, therefore, to be designed. With this in mind, the EC Commission specified the fiscal and statistical information required for sellers and buyers to account for their purchases and sales to their respective national administrations in the Single Market trading environment.

Statistical information on intra-EC trade is provided by Supplementary Declarations, (INTRASTAT) which are submitted by EC traders to their own national administrations on a regular basis.

Fiscal information is covered by the requirement for EC sellers and buyers to record details of all their purchases and sales within the Single Market on EC Sales Lists (ESLs). In the new trading environment the terms "imports" and "exports" have become redundant, and intra-Community transactions are now more familiarly known as "supplies" and "acquisitions". This has meant that buyers purchasing goods from sellers registered for VAT in other EC countries no longer have to pay tax at the time goods are imported. VAT is accounted for on "acquisition" of the goods and detailed on the relevant national VAT return form at the end of the accounting period.

Further information on Supplementary Declaration and EC Sales Lists has been given in Chapter 2 of this book[3].

Effects on the use of Incoterms

Where Incoterms are used in the trade of goods within the Single Market, a number of consequences may ensue on such usage.

a) The most singular effect of the Single Market on Incoterms usage is in respect of the seller/buyer obligations for completing customs formalities, which are covered by articles A2 and B2 of Incoterms 1990. This, of course, only covers one out of the ten seller/buyer obligations laid down by Incoterms.

However, even under the Single Market, articles A2 and B2 may still apply because the abolition of customs formalities at internal frontiers does not exempt sellers and buyers from licensing or official authorization requirements for strategic goods (which still need to be accompanied by official documentation) and other goods which are purchased from non-EC member states. Such goods are said to become in free circulation within the Community only if the following requirements[4] have been satisfied:

(i)   if import formalities have been complied with and

(ii)   if any customs duties or charges having equivalent effect which are payable have been levied and

(iii)   if they have not benefited from a total or partial drawback of such duties or charges.

EC sellers and buyers should thus be aware that there are a number of areas in which Single Market transactions should not be treated on entirely the same basis as domestic sales. Goods subject to excise controls also fall within the category of goods not in free circulation.

b)   Prior to 1 January 1993, the necessary documentation for transit movements was generally raised at the same time as export clearance documentation. Indeed, the SAD was specifically designed to fulfil export, transit, and import functions. However, in the Single Market environment, the seller no longer has to complete export formalities for goods consigned to other EC countries. The buyer, therefore, needs to be aware, particularly when using "F"-and "C"-category incoterms, that any transit documentation the buyer may require will be his responsibility and cost.

c)   The Single Market is also quite obviously not yet a domestic market for VAT purposes. VAT for registered traders is accounted for by an acquisition procedure within a destination based VAT system. Thus, transparency of supply has yet to be fully achieved, which means it is not yet possible to account for sales to EC customers on the same basis as buyers trading in the seller's own domestic market.

Clearly, transparency of supply is the ultimate goal to work towards in order to create a truly domestic market within the EC. Work has begun on this front, with proposals for a definitive-origin-based system currently being developed by the EC Commission. If the original timetable is implemented, VAT should be accounted for at origin from about 1997; but some doubts exist that this timetable will be met.

However, whilst VAT continues to be acquisition-based, sellers will have to consider how best to obtain the proof of goods leaving the country required to benefit from exemption of the payment of VAT. Before the Single Market a certified export SAD or certificate of shipment provided the necessary proof. However, this procedure has been considerably simplified as valid commercial evidence can be used to prove that goods have left the seller's country.

The need for Incoterms in the single market

The introduction of the Single Market has changed the way that EC traders have traditionally operated. The abolition of internal frontiers and official formalities has perhaps created a perception in some quarters that Incoterms are suitable only for international trade operations with non-EC countries. However, import and export clearance are just one element of an international sales contract. The division of the costs and risks associated with the delivery of goods between sellers and buyers remain a very important element of any sale. The division of these responsibilities is applicable to all trade, notwithstanding its domestic, Community, or international nature.

Given this factual situation, the use of Incoterms remains valid not only in the Single Market but also relevant to equivalent trading blocks elsewhere in the world.

Moreover, at present EC consumers do not have any recourse to a Community-based Sale of Goods Act. Rules concerning the transfer of title as well as the transfer of risks vary from country to country within the EC. So although borders may have disappeared for the purposes of customs formalities, the laws covering the sale of goods will not necessarily be the same in each Member State. One of the consequences of the gradual evolution of national legislation according to the customs and traditional background of individual

EC countries is that this has resulted in some variations in the interpretation of contract law. The existence of clearly defined incoterms which can transcend such national barriers and provide transparent delivery terms is therefore just as important in the Single Market trading environment.

As discussed earlier, EC sellers and buyers must still negotiate responsibilities for the carriage of the goods and divide the associated costs and risks accordingly. Various international conventions have been developed over the years dealing with the transport of goods and the necessary accompanying documentation. At EC level, rules governing the transport of goods are referred to in the Treaty of Rome[5], the Single European Act of 1986[6], the Maastricht Treaty[7] and Regulation 4056/86. None of these pieces of legislation, however, address whether an intra-Community movement can be treated as domestic carriage. This is obviously an area which requires legal clarification. In the meantime, Incoterms can quite clearly perform the initial task of specifying the place, time, and conditions of delivery for goods moving between sellers and buyers based in different EC countries.

Incoterms are also still required for the completion of the official returns demanded by national administrations to account for revenue and statistics arising from intra-EC trade. Prior to 1 January 1993 the Single Administrative Document was used for this purpose and details of the delivery terms used was part of the information required for official purposes at the frontier[8]. The EC Commission decided that statistical information regarding the incoterms used would still be required for official purposes. This is catered for by including a box on the Supplementary Declaration for Intrastats for describing the "delivery terms" used[9]. The Intrastat declaration has of course to be completed by the seller and buyer in their respective Member States and the EC Commission has stipulated that the delivery terms box of the return must show the relevant incoterm. Copies of the INTRASTAT forms in use in the UK are attached to this Chapter.

The introduction of the Supplementary Declaration for statistical purposes has therefore had quite a positive effect on EC traders' general awareness of the use of Incoterms. It is probably fair to say that larger companies with greater shares of markets in non-EC countries were reasonably familiar with the use of Incoterms anyway. Many smaller and medium companies have, by contrast, tended to deal only within the EC, and before the Single Market, they relied upon a third party agent such as a freight forwarder to complete the necessary customs formalities. Now, however, the onus is upon EC sellers and buyers to provide the necessary information for official purposes. In order to comply with these new requirements many traders have had to become far more familiar with the use of Incoterms as a matter of urgency. Greater familiarity with Incoterms will hopefully encourage their use within the EC on a more regular basis in place of some of the ad hoc and home-made terms that have been used over the years between EC trading partners. In this respect, the Single Market is a very good instrument which may bring about more widespread use of Incoterms.

However, in order to use Incoterms properly in the Single Market, it is necessary to understand the impact that the new trading environment has had on the individual terms. The main changes are described below.

Making the right choice

All 13 of the current incoterms can be applied to intra-EC trade deals, although, as we shall see, the DDU term was created to coincide with the introduction of the Single Market or any other equivalent grouping.

In Incoterms 1990, the different trade terms have been grouped in four categories, using the first letter as an indication of the group to which the term belongs. There is only one "E"-term (EXW), but there are three "F"-terms (FCA, FAS and FOB), four "C"-terms (CFR, CIF, CPT and CIP) and five "D"-terms (DAF, DES, DEQ, DDU and DDP). The first letter indicates the distinguishing characteristic of each of the latter three groups, viz.:

- "F" signifies that the seller must hand over the goods to a nominated carrier <u>F</u>ree of risk and expense to the buyer;

- "C" signifies that the seller must bear certain Costs even after the critical point for the division of the risk of loss of or damage to the goods has been reached;

- "D" signifies that the goods must arrive at a stated Destination[10].

The changes introduced to the way EC traders operate their business within the Single Market environment has meant that EC sellers and buyers should consider very carefully the appropriateness of the incoterms they use. This particularly applies to EC trading partners who may have dealt with each other over several years and have not re-examined their existing use of Incoterms regardless of the changed circumstances. They would be well advised to consider if the traditionally used incoterms still adequately covers both their needs and obligations to each other.

Buyers and sellers using Incoterms for intra-EC trade should bear some of the following points in mind.

EXW

The abolition of customs formalities at internal frontiers has meant that the seller no longer has to provide a transport document for presentation at the place of export from his own country. Prior to the Single Market the transport document was commonly used by the seller as proof that the goods had left the seller's premises for export. The current situation is that the seller must still provide proof that the goods have left his country in order to zero rate VAT for the supply of goods or services provided to buyers registered for VAT in other EC countries. In many cases this proof can continue to be provided by the transport document as the carrier will provide a certified copy of the transport document to the shipper, who when this term is used must be the seller. If a transport document is not available, other valid commercial evidence will be accepted by most EC countries as proof that the goods have been removed from the seller's country.

"F" category terms

As mentioned earlier, the buyer, instead of the seller, is now responsible for raising any official documents needed for the transit of goods through non-EC countries and the other circumstances in which transit documentation might be required, (such as goods still subject to transitional rates of duty or to strategic exports required to be under customs control until they reach their final destination).

FAS and FOB terms are only relevant for goods being carried by ship and should therefore only be considered when trading goods carried by sea is involved. FCA is, on the contrary, a multi-modal term. The Single Market does not relieve the seller of his obligations to obtain any required export licences or official authorizations. The seller still needs to provide evidence of delivery of the goods to the carrier nominated by the buyer. A copy of the transport document from the carrier, or alternative acceptable certificates can be used to provide the necessary proof.

"C" category terms

As above, the buyer will need to raise any necessary transit documentation[11]. It is thus the buyer who has to do whatever may be needed to pass the goods through a third country after they have been dispatched from the seller's country.

CFR and CIF terms are similar to FAS and FOB in that they are only suitable for goods being carried by ship. Sellers are still required in the Single Market trading environment to provide the necessary transport documentation and comply with any licensing or official authorization requirements in order to export the goods.

The multi-modal CPT and CIP terms also continue to place obligations on the seller to provide the necessary transport documents, licences, authorizations, etc.

"D" category terms

The DAF term is primarily used for through rail transport of goods[12] but it may be applied to any form of transport. It obliges the seller to deliver the goods for export at a named frontier, and to provide the necessary documentation to enable the buyer to take delivery of the goods. The seller has not only to bear the costs of transport to the named frontier, but also the risks of loss or damage to the goods. Although customs clearance formalities no longer need to be observed at the frontier, there are other reasons why goods might be held up, or possibly unloaded and then reloaded. One example of this is the differences in railway track widths between some EC countries, and this sort of factor should be borne in mind, particularly when deciding whether to use CPT or DAF terms.

The DES and DEQ terms make the seller responsible for the delivery of the goods to the named port of destination. If DES terms are used the buyer will still need to provide any necessary import licences or official authorisations. When DEQ terms are used it continues to be the seller's responsibility to provide any of the required export and import licences and official authorizations. The abolition of customs clearance formalities in the Single Market has not relieved the seller and buyer of the other obligations covered by Articles A2 and B2 of the relevant terms.

The DDU term is the only term that was specifically rephrased in 1990 to take account of the post 1992 trading environment. It was modified to take account of business demands from EC traders for a delivery term that would cater for the situation where VAT is accounted for on acquisition of the goods by the buyer. DDU is, therefore, particularly recommended for intra-EC trading whilst VAT is accounted for on acquisition of goods or services.

DDP on the other hand is not applicable to intra-EC trading at present as it places the onus of responsibility on the seller for payment of any import taxes, duty etc. However, this situation will need to be reviewed when the VAT origin based system is introduced.

Conclusion

As has been illustrated, Incoterms, with the exception of the DDP term, continue to be wholly applicable in the Single Market trading environment. EC traders need to consider several issues when considering the extent of the seller's and buyer's obligations to each other, and the abolition of customs clearance formalities at internal EC frontiers is just one small part of those obligations. The division of responsibilities for the carriage of goods from seller to buyer, and the costs and risks associated with this process are as relevant as ever. It is therefore strongly recommended that those involved in intra-EC trade should continue to negotiate delivery terms by using Incoterms.

The inclusion of Incoterms as part of the mandatory information that has to be supplied to national administrations through Intrastat Supplementary Declarations has had the positive effect of increasing EC traders' general awareness of their existence. In the long term, this can only be of benefit to the role that Incoterms can play in providing a level playing field for international trade. The more widely Incoterms are used, the easier it becomes for sellers and buyers to treat their international and national sales on the same basis, thus achieving the ultimate goal of transparency of delivery. The continuing growth of international trade and its importance to the wealth of individual nations provides an ideal opportunity for Incoterms to be used as an effective tool for encouraging best business practice between sellers and buyers.

We live in a fast changing world with commercial and technical progress being made at increasingly rapid rates. This may result in future changes to the current Incoterms. However, at this stage it is impossible to predict the extent to which Incoterms may have to be adapted to meet these new commercial and technical challenges.

The next major event that can be seen on the horizon and that will certainly have an effect on the use of Incoterms in the Single Market, will be the introduction of the origin based system for VAT. This will result in the DDU term becoming virtually redundant, whilst the current barely used DDP terms will become relevant once more. It is at this stage that articles A2 and B2 might need rephrasing to specifically mention official requirements in a Single Market environment.

It is clear that Incoterms, linked to the sales contract, have a vital role to play in ensuring that intra-community trade (and other equivalent regions such as NAFTA) is undertaken in the most efficient manner. This is because the delivery risk and cost element are fundamental to the contract.

Notes

1   ICC Publication no.460.

2   EEC Council Regulations No.678/85 and 679/85 of 18 February 1985 introduced the SAD to simplify formalities in trade in goods within the Community.

3   See Chapter 2, Incoterms and Documents.

4   Article 10(1) of the Treaty of Rome.

5   Title IV of Part Three (art.74-84) of the Treaty of Rome relates to Transport.

6   cf. article 16 of the Single European Act.

7   cf. article G(16) amending article 75 of the Treaty of Rome.

8   cf. specimen SAD documents annexed to EEC Commission Regulation No.2453/92 of 31 July 1992, OJ No. L.249/1.

9   This is so with regards to the two of INTRASTAT forms; cf. specimen forms annexed to EEC Commission Regulation No.3590/92 of 11 December 1992, OJ No. L.364/32. The UK has adopted only two of the three forms annexed to the abovementioned Regulation. Therefore, only these latter are attached to this chapter, in Appendix 1.

10 Guide to Incoterms, ICC Publication no.461, 1991, p.15.

11 cf. article B2, Incoterms 1990.

12 cf. Guide to Incoterms 1990, p.22.

INTRA EC TRADE STATISTICS

Supplementary Declaration

Trader. VAT No.	Branch ID	Official Use Only

Agent. VAT No.	Branch ID	

HM Customs and Excise

INTRASTAT

ARRIVALS | Period | No of items

1	1. Commodity code	2. Value £'s Sterling	3. Delivery terms	4. Nature of transaction	5. Net mass (kg)
	6. Supplementary units	7. Country of cons.	8. Mode of transport	9. Country of origin	10. No. of consignments	11. Trader's reference

2	1. Commodity code	2. Value £'s Sterling	3. Delivery terms	4. Nature of transaction	5. Net mass (kg)
	6. Supplementary units	7. Country of cons.	8. Mode of transport	9. Country of origin	10. No. of consignments	11. Trader's reference

3	1. Commodity code	2. Value £'s Sterling	3. Delivery terms	4. Nature of transaction	5. Net mass (kg)
	6. Supplementary units	7. Country of cons.	8. Mode of transport	9. Country of origin	10. No. of consignments	11. Trader's reference

4	1. Commodity code	2. Value £'s Sterling	3. Delivery terms	4. Nature of transaction	5. Net mass (kg)
	6. Supplementary units	7. Country of cons.	8. Mode of transport	9. Country of origin	10. No. of consignments	11. Trader's reference

5	1. Commodity code	2. Value £'s Sterling	3. Delivery terms	4. Nature of transaction	5. Net mass (kg)
	6. Supplementary units	7. Country of cons.	8. Mode of transport	9. Country of origin	10. No. of consignments	11. Trader's reference

6	1. Commodity code	2. Value £'s Sterling	3. Delivery terms	4. Nature of transaction	5. Net mass (kg)
	6. Supplementary units	7. Country of cons.	8. Mode of transport	9. Country of origin	10. No. of consignments	11. Trader's reference

7	1. Commodity code	2. Value £'s Sterling	3. Delivery terms	4. Nature of transaction	5. Net mass (kg)
	6. Supplementary units	7. Country of cons.	8. Mode of transport	9. Country of origin	10. No. of consignments	11. Trader's reference

8	1. Commodity code	2. Value £'s Sterling	3. Delivery terms	4. Nature of transaction	5. Net mass (kg)
	6. Supplementary units	7. Country of cons.	8. Mode of transport	9. Country of origin	10. No. of consignments	11. Trader's reference

9	1. Commodity code	2. Value £'s Sterling	3. Delivery terms	4. Nature of transaction	5. Net mass (kg)
	6. Supplementary units	7. Country of cons.	8. Mode of transport	9. Country of origin	10. No. of consignments	11. Trader's reference

When complete return to:-
HM Customs and Excise, Tariff and Statistical Office,
Sort Section, Portcullis House, 27 Victoria Ave.,
Southend-on-Sea,
Essex, SS2 6AL.
Your declaration must be received by the 10th. working
day after the period end.

Place and date

Name of signatory (in BLOCK LETTERS)

Signature

C1500   CD3378/N4(11/92)   F8639 (Dec 92)

SUPPLEMENTARY DECLARATION: ARRIVALS

Notes

1. Detailed advice on how to complete this form and on the Intrastat system generally is to be found in Customs and Excise Notice 60. If you need further help please contact your local VAT office.

Continuation sheets (C1500 (cont)) are available.

2. This form must only be used for goods which have arrived in the United Kingdom from another European Community (EC) country. If you have to declare dispatches of goods to another EC country, you must use the Dispatches Supplementary Declaration form (C1501). These are obtainable from your local VAT office.

3. If you are declaring more than 177 items it would be helpful if you would submit them in batches of not more than 14 continuation sheets to each C1500 declaration.

4. Header Information

    a.   It is important that you quote your VAT number correctly, together with the name and address of your business. The 3 digit branch ID should only be completed where you have notified Customs and Excise Tariff and Statistical Office that you will be providing data on a branch basis and have already advised the Branch ID number to them.

    b.   The agent box should be completed where the declaration is being made by a third party, such as a freight forwarder, on behalf of the person legally responsible. Legal responsibility is covered in Notice 60.

    c.   The period is the month and year to which the declaration refers, e.g. 09/93 for September 1993. Where special Supplementary Declaration periods are used in order to align with non standard VAT accounting periods, the month to be shown will be that covering the greater part of the period.

    d.   The bold numbering against each item on the left of the form indicates the item number. The total number of items covered by the declaration should be entered in the 'number of items 'box immediately below the Intrastat logo.

5. Item Details

Customs and Excise have produced a book of codes to be used, including the commodity codings as laid down in the Combined Nomenclature of the European Community. This book should be used in conjunction with Notice 60.

This form should be completed by typewriter or other mechanical or automatic reproduction process.

The law requires that complete and accurate Supplementary Declarations must reach the address overleaf by the tenth working day after the period end. Failure to comply could render you liable to legal proceedings.

CD 3378/R/N4(11/92)   Printed in the UK for HMSO 12/92 D.8368329 C10,000. 36625

INTRA EC TRADE STATISTICS   **Supplementary Declaration**

Trader.	VAT No.	Branch ID	Official Use Only
Agent.	VAT No.	Branch ID	

H M Customs and Excise

INTRASTAT

DISPATCHES | Period | No of Items

	1. Commodity code	2. Value £'s Sterling	3. Delivery terms	4. Nature of transaction	5. Net mass (kg)
1	6. Supplementary units	7. Country of destination	8. Mode of transport	10. No. of consignments	11. Trader's reference

	1. Commodity code	2. Value £'s Sterling	3. Delivery terms	4. Nature of transaction	5. Net mass (kg)
2	6. Supplementary units	7. Country of destination	8. Mode of transport	10. No. of consignments	11. Trader's reference

	1. Commodity code	2. Value £'s Sterling	3. Delivery terms	4. Nature of transaction	5. Net mass (kg)
3	6. Supplementary units	7. Country of destination	8. Mode of transport	10. No. of consignments	11. Trader's reference

	1. Commodity code	2. Value £'s Sterling	3. Delivery terms	4. Nature of transaction	5. Net mass (kg)
4	6. Supplementary units	7. Country of destination	8. Mode of transport	10. No. of consignments	11. Trader's reference

	1. Commodity code	2. Value £'s Sterling	3. Delivery terms	4. Nature of transaction	5. Net mass (kg)
5	6. Supplementary units	7. Country of destination	8. Mode of transport	10. No. of consignments	11. Trader's reference

	1. Commodity code	2. Value £'s Sterling	3. Delivery terms	4. Nature of transaction	5. Net mass (kg)
6	6. Supplementary units	7. Country of destination	8. Mode of transport	10. No. of consignments	11. Trader's reference

	1. Commodity code	2. Value £'s Sterling	3. Delivery terms	4. Nature of transaction	5. Net mass (kg)
7	6. Supplementary units	7. Country of destination	8. Mode of transport	10. No. of consignments	11. Trader's reference

	1. Commodity code	2. Value £'s Sterling	3. Delivery terms	4. Nature of transaction	5. Net mass (kg)
8	6. Supplementary units	7. Country of destination	8. Mode of transport	10. No. of consignments	11. Trader's reference

	1. Commodity code	2. Value £'s Sterling	3. Delivery terms	4. Nature of transaction	5. Net mass (kg)
9	6. Supplementary units	7. Country of destination	8. Mode of transport	10. No. of consignments	11. Trader's reference

When complete return to:-
HM Customs and Excise, Tariff and Statistical Office,
Sort Section, Portcullis House, 27 Victoria Ave.,
Southend-on-Sea,
Essex, SS2 6AL.
Your declaration must be received by the 10th. working
day after the period end.

Place and date
Name of signatory (in BLOCK LETTERS)
Signature

C1501   CD3380/N4/(11/92)   F8640 (Dec 92)

SUPPLEMENTARY DECLARATION: DISPATCHES

Notes

1. Detailed advice on how to complete this form and on the Intrastat system generally is to be found in Customs and Excise Notice 60. If you need further help please contact your local VAT Office.

Continuation sheets (C1501 (Cont)) are available.

2. This form must only be used for goods which have been dispatched from the United Kingdom to another European Community (EC) Country. If you have to declare arrivals of goods from another EC country , you must use the Arrivals Supplementary Declaration form (C1500). These are obtainable from your local VAT office.

3. If you are declaring more than 177 items it would be helpful if you would submit them in batches of not more than 14 continuation sheets to each C1501 declaration.

4. Header Information

    a. It is important that you quote your VAT number correctly, together with the name and address of your business. The 3 digit branch ID should only be completed where you have notified Customs and Excise Tariff and Statistical Office that you will be providing data on a branch basis and have already advised the Branch ID number to them.

    b. The agent box should be completed where the declaration is being made by a third party, such as a freight forwarder, on behalf of the person legally responsible. Legal responsibility is covered in Notice 60.

    c. The period is the month and year to which the declaration refers, e.g. 09/93 for September 1993. Where special Supplementary Declaration periods are used in order to align with non standard VAT accounting periods the month to be shown will be that covering the greater part of the period.

    d. The bold numbering against each item on the left of the form indicates the item number. The total number of items covered by the declaration should be entered in the 'number of items' box, immediately below the Intrastat logo.

5. Item Details

Customs and Excise have produced a book of codes to be used, including the commodity codings as laid down in the Combined Nomenclature of the European Community. This book should be used in conjunction with Notice 60.

This form should be completed by typewriter or other mechanical or automatic reproduction process.

The law requires that complete and accurate Supplementary Declarations must reach the address overleaf by the tenth working day after the period end. Failure to comply could render you liable to legal proceedings.

CD 3380/R/N4 (11/92)   Printed in the UK for HMSO 12/92 D.8368331 C10,000. 36625

Problems Related to the FCA Term

BART VAN DE VEIRE

Introduction

FCA : general principles

The version of the FCA term adopted in Incoterms 1990 superseded the old FOR/FOT and FOB Airport terms contained in Incoterms 1980. Those terms had been directed at particular modes of transport; the FCA term in contrast is appropriate to all modes of transport where the seller performs his duty of delivery by handing over the cargo to a carrier nominated by the buyer.

The FCA term is to be preferred whenever the carrier takes over the goods before – often long before – they are loaded onto the means of transport agreed upon between buyer and carrier.

Expanding the FCA term to every mode of transport was necessary as a result of the growing use of a number of transport techniques such as unitized cargo (containers and swap-bodies), ro-ro techniques in short-sea transport, etc.

All these techniques are characterised by two essentials:

1. the goods are taken over by the carrier or someone acting on his behalf long before they are taken on board a ship, or loaded on a truck, wagon or aircraft;

2. if the goods are to be delivered to a terminal, the terminal operator will be working for account of the carrier and not for account of the seller or buyer.

These new techniques also resulted in the growth of terminal-to-terminal and door-to-door transport, under the different forms of multimodal transport.

Since it is the buyer who arranges the contract of carriage with the carrier, he has to specify the place or point and the date or period for delivery to the seller.

Determining where and when the delivery will take place is important, because under the "F"-terms the point of delivery is the place where risks and costs are divided between buyer and seller. Until delivery, all costs and risks are for the account of the seller; after delivery all costs and risks are to be borne by the buyer.

FOB-FCA : which to choose ?

Choosing the right incoterm for an international sale means that buyer and seller are looking for an incoterm which will make the contract of sale match with the contract of carriage. To match a contract of sale under an incoterm of the "F"-group with a contract of carriage, delivery under the sale contract must coincide with the handover of the goods to the carrier. To put it another way, the transfer of risks and costs between seller and buyer should happen at the same moment and point as the transfer of risks and costs between shipper and carrier.

If the parties have decided to use an "F"-term this implies that the buyer will bear the costs and risks of the main carriage, and that delivery will be completed when the goods have been handed over to the carrier nominated by the buyer.

Before choosing among the "F"-terms, buyer and seller should decide:

1. at which point delivery will take place (port/inland terminal/seller's premises)
2. which kind of transport technique will be used (multimodal or not, unitised or break-bulk)
3. under which terms the contract of carriage will be concluded (liner terms or free in[1]).

The answer to these questions will make clear where the goods are handed over to the carrier, from where the cargo is under custody of the carrier, and which costs are covered by the freight agreed upon in the contract of carriage.

In the Introduction to Incoterms 1990 it is clearly stated that the FOB term should only be used when the ship's rail is the critical point for handing over the goods to the carrier[2]. Whenever the seller is called upon to hand over the goods to the carrier or a terminal operator acting for the carrier's account before the ship arrives at the loading port, the parties are advised to use the FCA term instead of the FOB. The main reason for this is that where goods delivered to a terminal are sold on FOB terms, the seller would bear risks and costs after he surrenders control of the goods and after he relinquishes any right as to their custody.

Since the introduction of Incoterms 1990, FCA and the allocation of terminal handling charges (THC) have been at the centre of discussion between buyers and sellers.

To be able to answer the central question – who should pay for the THC at the point of delivery? – two problems need to be addressed:

1.   where does delivery take place under FCA?

2.   what are the exact contents of the term THC?

Only after we have an answer to these two problems can we come to our conclusion, i.e. how to avoid a dispute over THC.

1   Delivery under FCA

1.1   Definition

1.1.1   General principles

Delivery under the FCA term takes place when the seller delivers the goods into the custody of the carrier named by the buyer, at the named place or point on the date or within the period agreed for delivery and in the manner agreed or customary at such point[3]. The duty to deliver the goods to the carrier does not imply that the seller can only rightly deliver the goods to the carrier himself. Delivery is also effected when the cargo is put into the custody of a terminal operator, or anybody else working for account of the carrier nominated by the buyer[4].

Given that the FCA term is intended to be used with any mode of transport, implying that the delivery for carriage will happen at different points to different types of carrier operating under widely different conditions, the Working Party preparing the Incoterms 1990 chose to set forth in FCA, article A4, only the general principles determining when delivery to the carrier is completed in particular circumstances. It should be tolerably clear to the seller, from the mode of transport and from the carrier's receiving point, when delivery is completed under the contract of sale – and therefore when risk passes – through delivery to the carrier. However, in the ideal situation, parties would avoid all confusion by identifying in the contract of sale the precise point of delivery, e.g.

the carrier's cargo terminal, and whether the cargo should be containerised or not.

1.1.2 Different modes of transport

As abovementioned, "free carrier" means that the seller fulfils his obligation to deliver when he has handed over the goods, cleared for export, into the charge of the carrier named by the buyer at the named place or point on the date or within the period agreed for delivery and in the manner agreed or customary at such point[5]. According to article A4 FCA of Incoterms 1990, if no specific point has been agreed, and if there are several points available, the seller may select the point at the place of delivery which best suits his purpose. Failing precise instructions from the buyer, the seller may deliver the goods to that carrier in such a manner as the transport mode of that carrier and the quantity and/or nature of the goods may require. Article A4 goes on to specify, for each mode of transport, when delivery is deemed to be completed:

(i) Rail transport

When the goods constitute a wagon load, or a container load carried by rail, the seller has to load the wagon or container in the appropriate manner. Delivery is completed when the loaded wagon or container is taken over by the railway or by someone acting on its behalf.

When goods do not constitute a wagon or container load, delivery is completed when the seller has handed over the goods at the railway receiving point or loaded them into a vehicle provided by the railway.

(ii) Road transport

When loading takes place at the seller's premises, delivery is completed when the goods have been loaded on the vehicle provided by the buyer. When the goods are delivered to the carrier's premises, delivery is completed when they have been handed over to the road carrier or someone acting on his behalf.

(iii) Transport by inland waterway

The same distinction concerning the completion of delivery is made as in road transport.

(iv)   Sea transport

When goods constitute a full container load (FCL), delivery is completed when the loaded container is taken over by the carrier. When the container has been carried to an operator of a transport terminal acting on behalf of the carrier, the goods shall be deemed to have been taken over when the container has entered into the premises of that terminal. When the goods are less than a container load (LCL)[6], or are not be containerised, the seller has to carry them to the transport terminal. Delivery is completed when the goods have been handed over to the sea carrier or someone acting on his behalf.

(v)   Air transport

Delivery is completed when the goods have been handed over to the air carrier or someone acting on his behalf.

(vi)   Unnamed transport / Multimodal transport

In the case of unnamed or multimodal transport, delivery is completed according to the rules applicable to the transport mode during which the goods have been handed over.

From the above extract from FCA, article A4, it becomes clear that the completion of delivery is synonymous with handing over the goods to the carrier or someone acting on his behalf. In most of the cases the handing over of the goods will mean that the seller will have to unload the goods at the carrier's premises to complete delivery.

There are only 3 exceptions to this rule:

1.   In rail transport, full wagon or container loads have to be loaded in the wagon or container by the seller, and delivery is only completed when the loaded wagon or container is taken over by the railway. In the case of a container to be carried by rail, this implies the unloading of the container at the railway's terminal, provided this is the named point of delivery.

2.   When loading takes place at the seller's premises (i.e. if the seller's premises are the named point of delivery), delivery is completed when the loading of the vehicle, container or inland waterway vessel provided by the buyer, is completed.

3.   In the case of a full container load (FCL) to be carried over sea which has to be carried to a terminal operator acting on behalf of the sea carrier, the sea carrier shall be deemed to have taken over

the goods when the container has entered into the premises of that terminal. This means that delivery is completed when the vehicle carrying the container has passed the terminal's gate.

1.2 Who is a carrier?

In the introduction to the FCA term[7], Incoterms 1990 give a clear definition of the term "carrier":

"'Carrier' means any person who, in a contract of carriage, undertakes to perform or to procure the performance of carriage by rail, road, sea, air, inland waterway or by a combination of such modes."

It is clear that the term "carrier" not only refers to a person or enterprise actually performing the carriage, but also to a person or enterprise undertaking to perform or to procure the performance of the carriage, provided that he assumes liability as a carrier for the carriage agreed upon. So a freight forwarder issuing a negotiable FIATA Multimodal Transport Bill of Lading is to be considered as a carrier.

On the other hand, since it is the buyer who has to instruct the seller to whom the goods have to be delivered, the buyer might nominate a person, e.g. a freight forwarder or a warehouse operator, who is not a carrier (i.e. someone who doesn't assume the liability of a carrier). The question then arises whether the seller effects delivery – and transfers risk – by giving the goods to the person who, albeit not a carrier, has been nominated as such by the buyer. It would appear that in these circumstances, the seller does indeed deliver by handing over the goods to the person nominated as carrier by the buyer[8].

It is also obvious that the seller can discharge his duty to deliver the goods by handing them over to the carrier himself. The goods can as well be handed over to someone acting on behalf of the carrier, such as a terminal operator (sea transport), a handling agent (air transport), etc. As it is stated in the "Guide to the Incoterms 1990"[9], this may seem superfluous, but the ICC chose to make this clarification, in order to avoid any unnecessary misunderstandings.

2 THC

2.1 Definition

Generally speaking, Terminal Handling Charges[10] or THC refer to all charges related to the handling of cargo at the terminal of loading or discharging, operated by or for the account of the carrier.

These charges may be part of the freight agreed upon between shipper and carrier, or the carrier may choose to bill all or part of the THCs separately.

Whether THCs are entirely, partly or not at all part of the freight differs according to the transport mode used. Even within one transport mode regional differences, as well as differences among individual terminals, may exist. Also the names under which all or part of THCs are separately charged are diverse, such as THCs, Container Services Charges, Portliner Term Charges, Equipment Handover Charges[11], LO-LO charges[12], etc. In Annex 1, a number of these charges are defined.

In a more narrow, maritime sense, THCs are defined as "charges payable to a shipping line either for receiving a full container load at the container terminal, storing it and delivering it to the ship at the load port or for receiving it from the ship at the discharge port, storing and delivering it to the consignee"[13].

In the container shipping industry THCs have been taken a step further. Where goods are carried by sea under contracts providing for the carriage of full container loads, the goods are frequently carried in containers owned or leased by the carrier: here, the contract of carriage will also involve a number of handling operations at container depots, where consignors have to pick up an empty container prior to loading it, or where consignees have to return the empty container after discharging it.

In 1990, the ESC (European Shippers Council) and CENSA/ICWP (Council of European and Japanese National Shipowners Associations/Inter Conference Working Party) reached an agreement on the contents of the THC. The agreement resulted in a split-up of all costs related to the handling of the container into 80% for the shippers' account and 20% for the shipowners' account.

In a detailed study by Ruytjens[14], a total of 17 items were mentioned as terminal cost elements for the handling of General Cargo Containers at the port or terminal of loading. This study gives a clear picture of the number of moves involved in the handling of containers on a terminal. It should be clear that THCs never account for any cost of transport outside the terminal. Neither do they refer to any operations concerning the stuffing or stripping of a container. This is either done by or for account of the cargo interests or, when they are done by or for account of the carrier, the levy is referred to as CCC-charges.

2.2 How does THC fit in the allocation of costs under FCA?

It is clear from what has been said that THCs cover a complexity of terminal handling operations. As a result, when THCs are charged separately from the freight, the question arises as to who will have to bear them if buyer and seller agreed on a contract of sale FCA Incoterms 1990.

At first sight, the answer appears to be simple. Articles A6 and B6 of the FCA Incoterms stipulate:

A6 **"The seller must**
  • subject to the provision of B6;
  • pay all costs relating to the goods until such time they have been delivered to the carrier in accordance with A4."

B6 **"The buyer must**
  • pay all costs relating to the goods from the time when they have been delivered in accordance with A6."

So the essential point in deciding who is to pay the THC is to determine whether the THCs are costs related to handling operations taking place not later than delivery or rather after delivery has been completed.

As long as terminal handling charges reflect the costs of terminal handling operations effected not later than the completion of delivery to the carrier, the answer is fairly simple. In such cases, the terminal handling charges, or whatever they are called in that particular mode of transport or trade, will be for account of the seller.

If on the other hand the terminal handling charges cover only costs of terminal handling operations effected after delivery to the carrier, it is obvious that, under an FCA sale, these costs are for account of the buyer.

But whenever the THC reflect the cost of terminal handling operations effected not only prior to but also after delivery to carrier has taken place, as is the case with the THCs as they are known in the maritime transport of FCL-containers, there is a problem. For here it would appear that THCs applied by maritime carriers in the transport of FCL containers cover costs related to handling operations which under the FCA term fall partly on the seller and partly on the buyer. But how is the division of costs to be made?

Two possibilities to solve this problem can be discarded straight away, because they require a change in the contract of carriage, and consequently intervene in the relation between carrier and shipper.

The first of these possibilities is to include THCs in the freight. An immediate practical difficulty is that whereas the freight is normally expressed in e.g. US dollars, the THCs covering local costs in the terminal of loading or discharging are generally expressed in a local currency. Furthermore, an all-in freight diminishes the transparency of the costs of transport. Since THCs can differ substantially within a range of ports, such as the Hamburg-Bordeaux range, cargo interests are of course keen to keep THCs as a separate cost, so they can ship from the most competitive port.

Another strictly theoretical possibility would be the actual split-up of the THCs into a pre-delivery THC and a post-delivery THC, with the former to be paid by the seller and the latter by the buyer. Even if the carriers were able to make a split-up of the THCs in a pre-delivery THC and a post-delivery THC, it is difficult to see why they should be willing to do so. Carriers consider the THCs as part of the contract of carriage and are not likely to amend the THCs to solve a problem which to them is just a problem between cargo interests, i.e. the seller and the buyer.

So if THCs are not likely to be included in the freight, nor to be divided into a pre- and post-delivery THC, the ultimate solution to the problem of who is going to pay the THC lies in agreeing in the contract of sale, beyond dispute, who will bear the THC.

3 Conclusion: how to avoid a dispute over THC?

It has been said before that choosing the right incoterms means that the terms and conditions of the contract of sale should match those of the contract of carriage. More specifically for incoterms of the "F"-group, the transfer of costs and risks between seller and buyer should happen at the same moment and in the same place as the transfer of costs and risks between shipper and carrier.

Handling the problem of THC under the FCA term requires that two questions be answered:

1. Provided that seller and buyer know how the main carriage is going to be organised and where delivery to the carrier is going to take place, is it equally clear at what point exactly delivery is to be completed under the FCA term?

2. Have the seller and buyer agreed on the exact contents of the THC or similar charges?

The answer to these two questions may reveal that the allocation of the THC is no problem at all, since the THC cover only costs which refer to terminal handling operations taking place no later than delivery or after delivery has been completed. In the former case the THC are for account of the seller, in the latter case they are to be borne by the buyer.

A solution is only needed when the THC cover terminal handling operations which take place before delivery as well as after delivery. Several possibilities exist to cope with such situations.

3.1 A specific agreement

If seller and buyer are aware that there is only one specific well-known charge on which they have to agree, they can stipulate for the allocation of that charge to either buyer or seller by express clause. Provided that all other costs are without dispute, to be borne by seller or buyer, specific agreement may be the easiest and clearest solution.

3.2 Customs of the trade or port

It may not be necessary to make a specific agreement in order to deal with the allocations of THC or similar costs. In some trades or ports customs can exist which can solve this problem, because according to these customs THC or similar cost are to be borne by either seller or buyer. So, if seller and buyer agree with the allocation of costs according to the customs of the trade or the port, this problem can be solved without resorting to a specific agreement.

3.3 An addition to FCA

Seller and buyer may feel that an agreement on one specific type of charge related to terminal handling operations is not enough to deal with the allocation of all types of THC and similar charges on costs. Therefore they may opt for an amendment or addition to the FCA term, which would deal in general terms with all costs relating to terminal handling operations, especially when these charges cover operations prior to and after delivery under the FCA term has been completed.

With THCs levied in connection with FCL containers carried by sea in mind, the ICC Working Party on Trade Terms had worked out an addition to FCA which solves exactly this problem. Bearing in mind that neither the place of delivery nor the transfer risk had to be modified, the proposed addition is meant to create only an exception to the ruling of FCA, A6(1) and B6(1).

FCA, *A6*: **"The seller must**
subject to the provisions of B6
pay all costs relating to the goods until such time as they have been delivered to the carrier in accordance with A4."

FCA, *B6*: **"The buyer must**
pay all costs relating to the goods from the time when they have been delivered in accordance with A4."

The aim of the FCA addition is to have all costs related to terminal handling operations, which are charged to the goods, to be borne by the seller. The FCA addition reads as follows: **"FCA costs up to ship's side for seller's account unless included in freight."**

Depending on the circumstances or customs in the port of delivery or trade concerned, an equivalent for the term "ship's side", such as "ship's tackle" can be more appropriate. In any case, this FCA addition should be able to solve all problems concerning the allocation of any charge related to the terminal handling operations.

The purpose of this chapter was to make clear to the international trade community that the problems related to THC under FCA can be solved and that FCA is indeed to be preferred over FOB whenever a seller has to fulfil his obligation to deliver the goods by handing over the goods to the carrier (named by the buyer) not at ship's rail but at a cargo terminal before the ship or the vehicle has arrived at the loading port.

Annexes

Annex 1 – Terminology

On the terminal various costs are levied upon the goods for certain handling operations relating to the container.

Usually the Terminal Operator invoices these costs to the shipping line or via the shipping agent (for account of the sea carrier) who, then, will invoice this cost further to the shipper/consignee.

Therefore it is important that parties are aware of these costs so that they can specify them in their contracts and agree on "who is going to pay what" in order to avoid further problems.

Terminal handling charges (THC)

Terminal handling charges are charges levied for the handling of the container at the terminal in case of shipment per seagoing vessel or reception of a container out of seagoing vessel.

It is the Terminal Operator who invoices terminal charges including the loading operator to the shipping agent for account of the line.

Of the total costs which are levied on the terminal, Terminal Handling Charges are calculated on a cost split of 80% for the shipper and 20% for the carrier.

Since THC have become a common custom of the port, practitioners have to deal with it. The terminology of THC can vary: also terms like CHC (Container Handling Charges), CSC (Container Service Charges) are used. The choice between these terms will depend on the rules and regulations of the shipping conference and/or shipping line.

LCL (Less than container load)

In principle LCL charges cover the costs of stripping, that is to say stowage and destowage of the goods in and out of the container. For the carrier they are a partial recovery of the discharging and terminal costs, which are paid by the line to the stevedore or terminal operator. In normal cases these costs are included in the seafreight under liner terms, which means that the carrier has the obligation to keep the goods at the disposal of the ship's tackle to the third holder of the bill of lading. In case of inbound cargo in some ports separate regulations deal with reception charges.

LO/LO charges (lift on/lift off charges)

The lift on/lift off charges cover the charges to put the container on/off the vehicle.

Equipment Handover charges

These charges are brought in account by some carriers/operators when the container and/or the chassis is transferred to a third party.

This is mostly the case when the shipper or consignee or the freight forwarder representing the consignee, organise the carriage of the container and also the delivery or collection of the container at the terminal used by the shipping line.

Equipment surcharges

Where carriers or operators have to handle special types of containers, such as non-standard, side-door, multi-door, ventilated, open-top, folding, dry or liquid bulk, reefer containers, they will require surcharges because of the higher sums of money they need in order to perform the operations of loading or unloading.

Additional charges may be required for certain operation, such as plugging a reefer container.

Annex 2 – Rutjens' List of Terminal Cost Elements

Terminal Cost Elements General Cargo
Containers-export:

01 Delivering empty container and receiving full container at the terminal, and all clerical work and reporting associated with delivering and receiving.

02 Inspection and reporting condition of container and completion of interchange receipt.

03 Inspection and reporting of seals and wiring including removal of invalid labels and resealing as appropriate.

04 Movement of container on/from chassis, barge or railcar.

05 Internal transport of container from/to/from stack.

06 Handling container out off/into/out of stack.

07 Reporting of chassis, barge and railcar activities in/out of the terminal.

08 Storage of full container within the time limits defined in the conference tariff.

09 Take laden box out of stack.

10 Internal transport of container from stacking area to ship's side under hook.

11 Move of container from ship's side under hook to ship's rail.

12 Move of container from ship's rail into ship's cell (including ship's hold or deck).

13 Opening and closing of hatch covers including unsecuring and securing and movement of hatch covers from bay to bay or to quayside and vice versa.

14 Lashing of container.

15 Wharfage charges and quay dues etc. where related to cargo.

16 Physical and clerical terminal planning plus reporting of container activities into vessel, including damage reporting and inspection of seals, wiring and labels.

17 Overtime or public holiday extra working costs.

Terminal Cost Elements Temperature controlled containers – 2.8.89

The following elements are additional to GP containers and can either be incorporated into the GP cost to produce an average THC, or can be used to justify a higher THC for temperature controlled cargo.

18   Pre-trip container inspection

19   Connecting of container cables, clip-on units and/or generating sets.

20   Electric power supply liquid nitrogen etc...

21   Monitoring of temperatures.

22   Administration including reporting of defective units and reporting equipment into/out of terminal.

23   Temperature controlled container costs in excess of GP items 8, 9, 10, 11 and 12.

24   Temperature controlled container costs in excess of GP items 13 and 18.

Terminal Cost Elements for Non-standard ISO containers

The following element is additional to GP containers and can either be incorporated into the GP costs to produce an average THC, or can be used to justify a higher THC for special containers.

25   For loading overheight or other non-standard containers involving the use of special spreaders or equipment.

Terminal Cost Elements for Dangerous cargo

The following element is additional to GP containers and can either be incorporated into the GP costs to produce an average THC, or can be used to justify a higher THC for containers carrying dangerous cargo.

26   Additional physical and administrative costs associated with the handling of dangerous goods (IMO) at terminals.

Uncontainerisable cargo and non-ISO containers

Note. Physical and administrative costs associated with the handling of non-iso containers or uncontainerisable cargo will be charged separately to a THC.

N.B.   The cost split of 80% for the shipper and 20% for the carrier and the calculation of the THC is based on these terminal cost elements.
Items 1 to 11 and 15 – for account of the cargo
Items 12 to 14 – for account of the ship
Items 16 and 17 – to be equally divided.

Notes

1. The terms "liner terms", "free in and out" and "free in" can be used differently by different people. For the purposes of this article, I refer to the definitions given by P.R. Brodie in the second edition of Dictionary of Shipping Terms:

   Liner terms:
   "qualification to a freight rate which signifies that it consists of the ocean carriage and the cost at the loading and discharging ports according to the customs of that port. This varies widely from country to country and, within countries, from port to port; in some ports, the freight excludes all cargo handling costs while in others the cost of handling between the hold and the ship's rail or quay is included".

   Free in and out:
   term qualifying a freight rate which signifies that it excludes the cost of loading and discharging and, if appropriate to the type of cargo, stowing, dunnaging, lashing and securing or trimming, all of which are payable by the charterer, or shipper or receiver as the case may be.

   Free in:
   free of expense to the shipowner of cargo handling at the loading port.

2. ICC Publication no.460, p.10; see also the introduction to FOB on p.39.

3. FCA, article A4, Incoterms 1990, p.26.

4. See Guide to Incoterms, page 54.

5. FCA explanation, Incoterms 1990, p.24.

6. For a definition of LCL, see Annex 1.

7. ICC publication 460, pp.24-25.

8. The introduction to FCA, in Incoterms 1990, page 25: "If the buyer instructs the seller to deliver the cargo to a person, e.g. a freight forwarder who is not a "carrier", the seller is deemed to have fulfilled his obligation to deliver the goods when they are in the custody of that person."

9. ICC publication no.461/90, p.54.

10. It is the Terminal Operator who invoices terminal charges including the loading operation, to the shipping agent for account of the line. Of the total costs which are levied on the terminal, Terminal Handling Charges are calculated on a cost split of 80% for the shipper, 20% for the carrier. Since THC have become a common custom of the port, practitioners have to deal with it. The incidence of these charges depends on the rules and regulations of the shipping conference and /or shipping line.

11. Some carriers/operators in some trades levy a THC when the container and/or chassis is transferred to a third party. This mostly happens when the shipper, the consignee or the freight forwarder who represents him, organises the carriage of the container and delivers or picks up the container at the terminal used by the shipping line.

12. Lift on/lift off charges cover the charges to put the container off/on the vehicle.

13. Dictionary of Shipping Terms, P.R. Brodie, (2nd. ed.), page 183.

14. The detailed study by Mr. Rutjens was based on the proposal made by the CENSA/ICWP on the 2nd August 1989, as accepted by the ESC in its letter of the 7th December 1990. The details are worked out in Appendix 2.

Incoterms and Contracts of Carriage on Liner Terms

CARINE GELENS

Introduction

It should be stressed that Incoterms only relate to trade terms used in the contract of sale and thus do not deal with terms which may be used in contracts of carriage, particularly terms of various charterparties.

Parties to contracts of sale are advised to consider this problem by specific stipulations in their contracts of sale – and to inform one another duly of such customs when they negotiate the contract so that it is made as clear as possible.

Inevitably a certain interpenetration will occur between the different contracts comprised in an international movement of goods. Therefore, conditions of the contract of carriage will influence the content of the contract of sale: the terms of the carriage contract themselves form part of the obligations assumed by the parties to the contract of sale.

Thus, the contract of sale will contain special clauses clarifying the extent and spirit of the contract of carriage, bringing into close contact the contracts of sale and carriage without necessarily touching upon the obligations imposed by Incoterms.

For example, special clauses can be inserted into the contract of sale so that it is made as clear as possible how much time is available for the seller to load the goods on the ship or other means of conveyance provided by the buyer and further to specify the extent to which the seller would bear the risks and costs of the loading operations under the "F"-terms and of the discharging operations under the "C"-terms.

Classic illustrations of such special terms would include the following:

FOB Stowed

This means that the parties to the sale contract agree that the responsibility of the seller continues until the stowage of the goods is completed in the hold of the ship. The effect of this clause is to delay the passage of risk and costs from seller to buyer beyond the ship's rail, transferring both to the buyer on completion of the stowage.

CIF FO (Free Out)

This means that the buyer authorises the seller to conclude the contract of carriage on the most favourable terms and that the buyer pays for the discharging costs.

CIF landed

This means that the unloading costs including lighterage and wharfage costs are borne by the seller.

These terms are of interest not only to the carrier, but also to the insurer, the freight-forwarder and the financial institutions with whom the parties to the sale contract may come into contact within the other contracts making up the entire transaction. The freight-forwarder in particular plays a significant role in advising his principal accurately of the precise purpose and effect of these terms.

A contract of carriage is said to be concluded on "liner terms" where the loading and discharging costs are included in the seafreight and paid by the shipper, who could be either the seller or the buyer, depending on whether the sale contract has been concluded in "C"- and "F"-terms within Incoterms.

Analysis of Incoterms 1990 according to the mode of transport used

The following list indicates which incoterms are appropriate to each different type of transport which can be used for the carriage of goods sold.

Any Mode of	EXW	Ex Works (...named place)
Transport including	FCA	Free Carrier (...named place)
Multimodal	CPT	Carriage Paid To (...named place of destination)
	CIP	Carriage and Insurance Paid To (...named place of destination)
	DAF	Delivered at Frontier (...named place)
	DDU	Delivered Duty Unpaid (...named place of destination)
	DDP	Delivered Duty Paid (...named place of destination
Air Transport	FCA	Free Carrier (...named place)
Rail Transport	FCA	Free Carrier (...named place)
Sea and Inland	FAS	Free Alongside Ship (named port of shipment)
Waterway Transport	FOB	Free On Board (...named port of shipment)
	CFR	Cost and Freight (... named port of destination)
	CIF	Cost, Insurance and Freight (... named port of destination)
	DES	Delivered Ex Ship (... named port of destination)
	DEQ	Delivered Ex Quay (... named port of destination)

Specific reference to the contract of carriage

Contracts of sale sometimes refer to "liner terms" and to "customs of the port". Each of these two types of reference will be looked at in turn.

1 Liner Terms

Definition

Whereas international trade was in former days a marine adventure in which all the interested parties actively participated, this all changed when liner transport was organised on a regular basis between various seaports.

In liner transport, the shipping line has a fixed sailing date (for example, weekly, every two weeks, monthly) from each port they sail from, with cargo space being booked with the shipping line directly or through an agent.

Some definitions of "Liner Terms", as published in the professional literature, are given hereunder.

The term **"Liner Terms"** has a similar meaning to "gross terms" and means that the shipowner bears all the costs related to the cargo handling and carriage. If, in addition to the full operating costs of the ship, all other expenses, tally charters, etc. are for the owner's account the charter is a "gross charter" or fixture on **"Gross Terms"**. The expression "Gross Terms" is in more common usage and conveys that the cost of loading, stowing, trimming and discharging are for account of the vessel. The term "liner terms" may differ from "gross terms" in that gross terms refers to bulk cargo and tramp trades whereas liner terms generally relates to liner trades.

The alternative is FIO[1], FIOT[2], and FIOST[3] when the cost of loading, stowing, trimming and discharging are not for account of the vessel. The owner is obliged to cover all expenses from "hook to hook", that is, from the time the cargo comes within reach of its tackle until the cargo leaves the ship's tackle at the discharging port[4]. Whether gross terms or FIO terms apply, port charges are payable by the vessel on a voyage charter.

If a ship is freighted on **"Berth Terms"**, sometimes also called "liner terms", this means that the ship is loaded and unloaded in the way which is customary with the regular lines taking part in the traffic in question. These terms do not mean that no special conditions with regard to the rate, i.e. tariffs, of loading and discharging can be agreed upon in the charter. Generally speaking, these terms also imply that the loading and landing charges are for the carrier's account, whereas the shipper and/or the consignee pay the usual contribution to the loading and landing charges[5].

Applicable law and documents

Although sea transport in earlier days enjoyed unrestricted freedom of contract, this was changed by the introduction of the 1924 Brussels Convention, otherwise known as the Hague Rules.

The need to protect the buyer/consignee was the main reason for the introduction of mandatory rules. Further amendments have been made to the Hague Rules in 1968 by the Visby Protocol regarding the limitation of liability. The Hague-Visby Rules apply to contracts of carriage where the bill of lading is the transport document. From the moment a bill of lading is issued, these Rules apply.

The bill of lading is a negotiable instrument with a particular legal character. Only the holder of the bill of lading is entitled to the goods at the place of destination.

The transport document

Before Incoterms 1990, the usual document in proof of delivery was the bill of lading. This was – and still is – of particular importance when the cargo is sold at sea or if parties to the contract of sale have a documentary credit. In some instances, another carriage document needs to be tendered in addition to the bill of lading. Thus, in the case of charterparties, some charter forms contain a specific type of bill of lading; and bills of lading frequently contain a reference to a charterparty. In either case, Incoterms require that a copy of the charterparty should be tendered by the seller to the buyer. This duty is imposed to protect the buyer in the "C"-terms where the seller, who has to contract for carriage, could choose a relatively cheap freight with the risk that the cargo is in danger during the sea carriage.

The precise ambit of this duty has raised a query with the ICC Working Party on Incoterms. Was the duty imposed wherever the bill of lading contained any reference, however minor, to the charterparty; or did it only apply where the bill of lading tendered was a bill of lading intended for use in conjunction with a particular charterparty?

At a meeting of the Working Party, it was agreed that only if the seller tenders a bill of lading making a full reference to the charterparty, would he be under a duty to tender the charterparty. In other cases, where the bill of lading tendered simply sought to incorporate particular clauses of a charterparty, the seller will at most provide the buyer information with respect to discharging such as laytime and demurrage provisions contained in the charterparty[6].

Incoterms 1990 introduced a reference to transport documents other than bills of lading[7], for example, a negotiable bill of lading, a non-negotiable sea waybill, an inland waterway document. Even the replacement of the transport document by an EDI message is envisaged.

All the abovementioned transport documents may quite easily be used under Incoterms instead of the traditional bill of lading, except where the buyer wishes to sell the goods in transit.

2 Customs of the port

A serious complication is created by the customs of the port.

These customs are the result of port techniques. The seller is not always allowed to deliver the goods alongside the ship or on board the seagoing vessel. These handling and loading operations are the task of the competent port authorities to whom the goods are to be handed over. Yet the seller may have certain obligations under the sale contract regarding such operations, with handling costs being incurred by the buyer only after the goods have been delivered by the seller to the carrier. Thus who is to bear handling costs and risks before shipment where the custom of the port disallows the seller from delivering the goods alongside or on board the vessel?

FOB and FAS

We will deal with the customs of the port in two maritime Incoterms which have already been in force for several years, namely FAS and FOB. The FOB term is probably the most used trade term of all incoterms. The FCA term is covered in Chapter 7 of this book, to which reference is here made.

FAS

The goods have to be delivered alongside the named vessel in a way that the ship's tackle is able to take the goods – or other instruments, landside or floating – to bring the goods on board.

Incoterms 1990 refer explicitly in article A4 to the customs of the port. This can oblige the seller to give the goods to the carrier (with whom he has no contractual relationship) or a designated third party who will bring the goods to the agreed point (for instance, the stevedore acting on behalf of the carrier or, in some ports, an official organisation). In this case, we can consider that the carrier or the third party handles at risk – and sometimes at cost – of the seller, as if it were he who delivered the goods.

This is, however, a controversial point of view[8]. A distinction could be made between who bears, on the one hand, the costs and, on the other hand, the risks. In most cases, customs of the port do not cause problems as to the handling costs. Usually, the cost of handling after the goods have been given by the seller is included in the seafreight, which is paid by the buyer.

However, there is still the question of who bears the risk. Who will take into account the loss (theft) of the goods within the period that the goods have been handed over to the carrier and before they are alongside the ship (or on board)? It could be argued that it should be the seller who bears the risk of such loss.

FOB

According to article A4 of FOB Incoterms 1990, the seller has to deliver the goods on board the vessel named by the buyer at the named port of shipment on the date within the period stipulated and in the manner customary at the port.

The customs of the port do not affect the general allocation of duties between the seller and the buyer under Incoterms 1990, but such customs will take into account detailed matters of costs. Thus, in certain ports, such as Antwerp, the customs of the port are defined in a resolution concerning the delivery of goods in the port of Antwerp.

FOB – Antwerp: an example

In Antwerp, the Antwerp Port Community (Agha) adopted a resolution in 1984 that supersedes all former resolutions, conditions and agreements which existed in the port of Antwerp.

The new resolution is divided into two chapters:

Chapter one deals with the relations between the maritime carrier and the shipper in the frame of the transport agreement. It contains stipulations regarding the delivery of the goods, the division of the costs and the transfer of risks between both parties for several kinds of cargo and methods of delivery, as well as the text of the uniform shipping permit of the port of Antwerp.

Chapter two regulates the rights and obligations, the division of costs and the transfer of risks between buyer and seller on the basis of the FOB – Antwerp agreement. We will analyse the situation of the delivery of normal goods and the apportionment of costs and transfer of risk under the Antwerp Liner Terms.

Chapter 1
1.   Delivery of goods
     On the quay. Normal goods, without extreme length and weight have to be deposited by the party delivering the goods at the place indicated by the sea carrier or his representative or in the latter's absence within the perimeter of the vessel.

By the term "perimeter" is to be understood the area within the confines of the bow and the stern of the vessel on the one hand, and the depth of the shed on the other, unless the sea carrier and/or the representative has indicated a different place. The distance on quays within sheds shall never be more than 120m from the vessel or that part of that distance bound by a public highway.

2. Apportionment of costs and transfer of risk.
    Delivery on the quay. Normal goods for conventional shipment.

The movement of goods from within the perimeter to under the ship's tackle is carried out by and at the expense of the sea carrier.

<u>Chapter 2</u>
Rights and obligations, apportionment of costs and risks between buyer and seller in the framework of the FOB – Antwerp contract of sale.

A FOB – Antwerp contract of sale may be based on:

*   specific terms in which the mutual obligations of the parties have been set out;
*   Incoterms;
*   the mere mention FOB – Antwerp;
*   the mention FOB – Antwerp with a reference to the relevant customs applications.

In the explanatory text, it is said that if a sale is concluded on the basis FOB incoterm, the goods will be delivered as laid down in section 1 of the resolution while the apportionment of cost and the transfer of risk will be settled on the basis of Incoterms.

To what extent does a FOB incoterm sale differ from a FOB – Antwerp sale? Whereas the crucial point in the FOB incoterm is the ship's rail, the critical point in FOB – Antwerp for the transfer of risk coincides with the transport agreement namely under the ship's tackle.

In Zeebrugge, a similar system is in force as a custom of the port.

Notes

1   Free in and out (chartering), cf. Kapoor, Peter, "The fairplay book of shipping abbreviations", 2nd. ed., 1993, Fairplay Publications Ltd., Surrey U.K., p.41.

2   Free in and out and trimmed (chartering), cf. Kapoor, Peter, op. cit., p.41.

3   Free in and out, stowed and trimmed (chartering), cf. Kapoor, Peter, op. cit. p.41.

4   Bes, J., "Chartering & Shipping Terms", Barker & Howard Ltd., 1992, at page 80.

5   Shipping Agency Practice by J.M. Van Berkum and W. Schuring.

6   Query 19, Summary Record 4.5.1993, Working Party on Trade Terms, ICC Paris, doc. no. 462/Int 114.

7   cf. articles A8 and B8 Incoterms 1990.

8   Handling costs are included in the freight. Nevertheless, the sea carrier is only liable from the moment the goods are slung under the ship's tackle. The risks of this movement within the perimeter are always borne by the buyer.

Variants on Incoterms (Part 1)

KAINU MIKKOLA

Standard variants – a must for Incoterms

The Incoterms 1990 Working Party has stated that the 1980 edition had not been adopted by the traders adequately, the main reason for that being its complexity. Therefore the aim of the Working Party was to simplify Incoterms.

In the 1990 edition of Incoterms, "Free Carrier" became de facto the master term; in its universality it was not only suitable to be taken as the working tool, but also to absorb the unwanted "uni-modal terms" – those for solely rail and air.

When designing the new FCA the key word was, naturally, the carrier. The buyer has two obligations concerning the carrier:
- firstly, to choose the carrier, and then
- to supply the seller with the carrier's name so as to enable the seller to effect delivery.

Consequently, the party nominated as carrier by the buyer to the seller was considered to be the carrier. This conclusion led to a hard but inevitable debate.

The reason for this debate is due to the fact that the name the buyer gives is often the name of a transport terminal. There are many modes of transport with terminals of their own type, and therefore many kinds of procedures which may need to be followed. To put them within one set of rules was – this was the opponents' main argument – not possible. That is what variants are needed for: to adjust the basic incoterms according to existing commercial practices.

Specific problems relating to the term FCA are dealt with in more detail in Chapter 7 of this book, reference to which is made.

1 Role of the ICC

The fact that one term may cover several types of procedures is no argument for expressly providing for such procedures within the standard Incoterms. The habitual phrase "in the customary manner" has solved this sort of problem before. Moreover, how could the ICC know in advance which situation would be worth covering?

Should the variants be left alone, to be evolved from practice? Or should the ICC take an active role from the very start?

There are several arguments in favour of the latter:

- If the variants are left to be conceived by practice, a bundle of variable clauses would arise, and sooner or later, the ICC would be asked to harmonize them. An active role from the start would lead to immediate uniformity.

- Such an active role would also make short code-like variants possible – their definitions being found in the text – a point which exponents in favour of the use of electronic data interchange (EDI) certainly would appreciate.

- Moreover, in such a case, the uncertainty of determining which situations are covered would not arise. Most of the needs to create variants were born, as stated above, through a wish to simplify matters. Thus, if a good system of introducing variants is evolved, new variants would be easy to add later on, when the need arises.

2 Main case – "FCA terminal..."

The difficulty that arises with the term "Free Carrier" is to find alternatives for different positions of the cargo around the terminal, such as "loaded from terminal onto departing vehicle". Such a specification would well fall within "at the named place or (specific) point" stipulated in Incoterms at FCA, article A4, and would thus not be in conflict with the basic rule.

As regards the point of delivery – by adjusting it within the delivery place – the variants would naturally cover the main obligations, action/costs and the risk.

2.1 Costs and risks in standard incoterms

The significance of a clear demarcation line for the transfer of risks and costs is fundamental to the entire layout of Incoterms. This demarcation line differs between the "E"-, "F"- and "D"-terms on the one hand and the "C"-terms on the other. In "E"-,"F"- and "D"-, costs and risks are not split, both passing to the buyer at the point stipulated by the chosen incoterm. In "C"-terms, on the other hand, risk passes at the point of departure, with costs being borne by the seller to the point of arrival. Just as the standard incoterms identify the point or points at which costs and risks pass, so should variants to Incoterms.

3　A variant to EXW

The call for variants to Incoterms came from Finland, not because of terminal problems, but because it was felt that there was a drastic risk gap at EXW. According to articles A4, A5 and B5 of EXW, risk passes to the buyer so soon as the goods are "placed at the disposal of the buyer at the named place of delivery on the date or within the period stipulated." Where a buyer's transport insurance gives cover from the point of actual delivery to the buyer, the buyer is left exposed to risks under the sale contract which are not covered by the insurance policy. Knowing how commonly EXW is used – because of its dominant role as the term of offer – this observation was a shock and gave birth to the idea of "EXW loaded".

This variant to EXW was initially met with an instinctive reluctance by Incoterms experts who wanted to respect the minimal character of the term. Consequently they would like to consider "loaded" as implying just an assistance of the seller to the buyer, which would not affect the risk. This would, however, leave the risk gap intact. It also would lead to splitting the obligations (see 2.1 above).

3.1　"EXW loaded" versus FCA

Experts have suggested that, if the purpose was to transfer risk at the point of delivery, the term FCA should be used rather than "EXW loaded". That used to be our instruction in the beginning until we came up against some obstacles.

Manufacturers with fixed price lists – based on EXW – with consignments regularly below the collection limit, such as producers of instruments, accessories etc. have been unwilling to give up EXW.

This reluctance is most concrete when the factory has a rural site. Distance to different transport terminals is long and variable and the costs to them bothersome to count, both per case and in average.

In such a case, the buyer will insist they add an over-estimated percentage for the FCA pre-carriage to be on the safe side.

3.2 "EXW loaded" versus "FCA seller's premises"

The next step was the proposal of the variant "FCA seller's premises". The question that now arises is which of the two terms – "EXW loaded" or "FCA seller's premises" is more logical and easier to be approved by the seller.

Even if "FCA seller's premises" would be more complete (including also the export clearance) it would be quite a (verbal) deviation from the seller's EXW; it is obvious that the seller would prefer just to add "loaded" to his EXW price lists.

This is because, firstly, "loaded" would be a familiar and safe concept to add, compared to going over to another term with a totally alien wording. Secondly, the operational changes for the seller would be minimal:

- His actions would stay at his own premises, within his existing internal traffic, and with control of the costs in his own hands. What is the difference of driving the fork lift with the pallet straight to the truck instead of leaving it at the loading pier? The only difference is timing.
- And above all, that is what he in fact has been doing all the time – who else would have been loading his EXW consignments?

Even if the same features exist at "FCA seller's premises", they are not explicitly said in the wording – a simplicity factor which affects both the seller and all the readers of the price list.

4 General aspects

4.1 Distortion of risk

It is a basic – and sound – principle of trade terms that the obligations are kept together: whoever has the custody of the cargo bears the risk. To deviate from that always means distortion and should be done only for special reasons. In standard Incoterms as well as in variants such deviation ought to be avoided lest new distortions are created. In Incoterms there are two types of such deviations from the norm:

- out of the regular terms, only the "C"-group term.
- in the case of assistance: if the seller renders the buyer assistance, at his request, such assistance takes place at buyer's risk and expense.

The variants should not be mistaken for assistance: while assistance is an action resulting from a specific request, variants are being designed for general use – that is why they should be standardised.

4.2   Terminology

Quite often the word "loaded" is used interchangeably with "loading" and the word "discharge" is used interchangeably with "discharging". When variants are used, greater precision is needed. While the word "loading" indicates the actual action of loading the cargo onto the means of transport, the cargo itself can only be said to be "loaded" when it is actually on the means of transport. The same can be said for discharge at the other end.

Therefore, where the parties intend to place the duty to load upon the seller, the variant used should specify "loading included" rather than "loaded" into their contract.

4.3   State of the cargo

The variants so far examined in this chapter dovetail nicely with Incoterms 1990 in that they simply seek to define the place of delivery of the goods. However, some variants describe not the place of delivery but the state of the goods on delivery. Thus, for example, goods may be described in the contract as "customs cleared"; the insurance relating to the goods may be described as "maximum cover"; and the packing of the goods may be described as "seaworthy packed". These variants go beyond simply defining the moment and place of delivery and therefore they also go beyond what is expressly provided for in Incoterms. This is inevitable given the many varied commercial circumstances in which parties operate.

5 Summary – The structure of variants of Incoterms

5.1 Variants concerning the position of the cargo

Where the variant simply seeks to define the position of the cargo on delivery, the variant chosen marks the moment at which the seller's obligations are performed. Such variants are "loaded", "terminal loaded", "undischarged" and are explained in the enclosed diagram.

On the other hand, where the variant seeks to allocate the costs of the action of loading, without affecting the passage of risk, the wording should be as follows: "loading (costs) excluded/included."

5.2 Variants concerning the state of the cargo

Where the variant refers to a particular feature of the goods on delivery, without seeking to alter the place at which the seller will be deemed to have delivered, then the variant will only cover the element mentioned. Therefore other obligations, be they customs clearance, insurance, packing, etc., will not be affected by the variant.

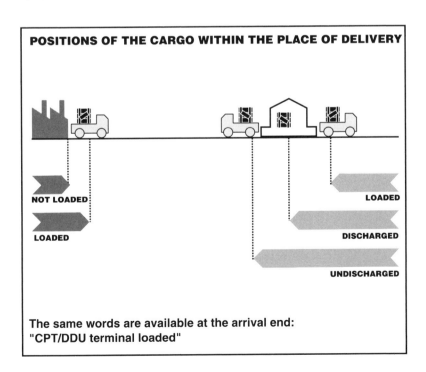

POSITIONS OF THE CARGO WITHIN THE PLACE OF DELIVERY

NOT LOADED

LOADED

LOADED

DISCHARGED

UNDISCHARGED

The same words are available at the arrival end:
"CPT/DDU terminal loaded"

Variants on Incoterms (Part 2)

ASKO RATY

Introduction

The seller and the buyer should know in advance each other's obligations – costs, risks and formalities – with sufficient accuracy. This is not always the case when general terms of trade, such as Incoterms 1990, are used. The purpose of the variants is to help the trading partners to conclude a business with success and without disturbance, in every detail. Parties may want to add something or delete something, in mutual understanding, to each other's obligations or they may feel it necessary to express something more precisely and exactly than the wording of the term itself allows.

The term "variant" means an addition to the basic term itself. It may add or delete the seller's obligations or, vice versa, delete or add the buyer's obligations.

Of all things which need to be defined in the contract of trade, delivery is the most important. Respectively, articles A4 and B4 are the most decisive, because they define the seller's obligation to deliver the goods and the buyer's obligation to receive the same. Division of costs and transfer of risks are in all other cases except "C"-terms bound simply to the definition when goods have been delivered.

The seller and the buyer may need to define the point of delivery more precisely, because the definition of delivery, especially the place of delivery, as given in article A4, is not always sufficiently detailed. Actually, it cannot be, by the very nature of the terms, which are supposed to fit into many circumstances.

If the users decide to specify the content of article A4, or more often a part of that article, this does not mean a change in the meaning of the term itself. It is a question of the specification of the delivery within the frames of article A4 as defined in the original wording of Incoterms 1990.

It is logical, especially from the point of view of common practice, that the party who performs or pays for the performance of something which is a part of the delivery, bears also the responsibility of the action in question, and the risk of damage to or loss of the goods.

If trading partners use an addition to Incoterms 1990 concerning delivery,

- the delivery as defined by articles A4 and B4 is not amended but only specified more precisely
- costs are divided and risk is transferred at the same place, again "C"-terms excluded.

The parties may agree that the seller pays some costs but does not bear the risk. In such a case parties may also use a variant, in which they state that only costs or risks are concerned. If the variant refers to the increase of costs, this means to the seller that he bears some costs on behalf of the buyer but that the transfer of risks is unaltered and the delivery of the goods is not affected. The seller is thus assisting the buyer. This is in accordance with the idea of mutual cooperation and with the appeal, which is often mentioned in Incoterms, calling the seller to render the buyer, at his request, risk and expense, every assistance in obtaining any documents etc.

The seller and the buyer may also agree that either party carries out some action, such as formalities, insurance , notice, packing etc. on behalf of the other party, or as an additional service. Such additions do not affect the delivery or the transfer of risks.

This chapter deals with some common variants, their meaning and their use. They are represented graphically at the end of the chapter. The seller and the buyer may also use other additions.

EXW loaded

Ex Works is seldom used properly as a term of delivery, although it is a common term of offer. The seller should have no obligations concerning the delivery of goods.

In EXW, loading of the goods is the buyer's responsibility.

However, it is often in the interest of the buyer to extend the seller's obligations until the goods are loaded on the vehicle. In such a case, the word "loaded" should be added to the term, e.g. "EXW Zoroza Incoterms 1990 loaded".

This variant moves the point of delivery and changes the seller's obligations to deliver the goods. The seller places the goods at the disposal of the buyer when they have been loaded on the vehicle at the named place. Thus the risks are transferred and costs re-divided at the same critical point.

EXW cleared, FAS cleared

According to EXW and FAS, the buyer must clear the goods for export. In both cases, however, the seller may want to take care of the export clearance.

In such a case, the word "cleared" can be added to the term, e.g. "EXW Lübeck Incoterms 1990 cleared" or "FAS Uddevalla Incoterms 1990 cleared".

Such variant does not affect the seller's obligation to deliver the goods or the buyer's obligation to take delivery of them. It only obliges the seller to obtain at his own risk and expense any export licence or other official authorisation, if any, and carry out customs formalities necessary for the exportation of the goods.

FCA undischarged, FCA loaded

According to FCA, article A4, the seller must "...deliver the goods into the custody of the carrier......". The seller may deliver the goods to the carrier by handing them over at his own premises, or by bringing the goods into the terminal and handing them over to the carrier.

In the case of terminal delivery it is not always clear when is the exact moment and where is the exact point of delivery.

That point may be:
- on the arriving vehicle, before discharging into the terminal;
- in the terminal itself;
- on the departing vehicle, when goods have been loaded for despatch.

Variants to Incoterms are needed to describe the situation, when goods are either on the vehicle, waiting for discharge, or on the vehicle, ready for despatch. Respective variants would be "undischarged" and "loaded". These variants define exactly the precise point of delivery.

It would be logical to consider that point also as the point where delivery is completed. Therefore risk is transferred and costs are divided at the same point, which is also the named point of delivery as per article A4.

The use of the addition "loaded" tells the seller that his obligations are extended through the terminal until the departing vehicle, e.g. "FCA Azuqueca Incoterms 1990 loaded".

The use of "undischarged" tells trading partners that the seller delivers the goods to the terminal, ready for unloading, e.g. "FCA Lübeck Incoterms 1990 undischarged". In such a case the buyer's obligations are extended to begin already at the moment goods are discharged from the arriving vehicle.

FOB stowed

FOB is the oldest term of delivery, reflecting the practice of the days of sailing ships. It is well-known and widely used. However, the definition of the delivery in FOB is by its nature not very exact. According to article A4, the seller must "deliver the goods on board ... in the manner customary at the port".

The seller may want to include in his delivery also some other measures, such as stowage or trimming. In such a case, the parties should use variants to describe the extension of the seller's obligations.

Examples of such variants are "stowed", "stowed and trimmed" and "stowed, trimmed and secured", e.g "FOB Rotterdam Incoterms 1990 stowed and trimmed". These variants do not affect the position of the goods and thus do not change the point of delivery and consequently the risk of the seller.

CIF maximum cover

According to Incoterms, the seller must obtain cargo insurance with minimum terms of the Institute Cargo Clauses (so called "C"-terms). In practice, however, parties usually insure deliveries with the widest possible terms, so called "A"-terms. The seller may describe this by using an addition "maximum cover", e.g. "CIF Felixstowe Incoterms 1990 maximum cover".

In such case, the insurance shall be in accordance with the maximum cover of the Institute Cargo Clauses (Institute of London

Underwriters) or any similar set of clauses added with the war and strike clauses.

The meaning of "maximum cover" may be a question of dispute. However, it is suggested that this should not cause too much difficulty in practice, as Institute Cargo Clauses "A" are widely used, and other clauses used in daily practice are very similar. If they want to be certain as to the cover procured, trading partners should name the precise clauses they require.

CFR/CIF undischarged

In the basic terms discharge is paid by the buyer, unless it is included in the sea freight payable to a regular shipping line. Trading partners may sometimes want to limit the seller's obligations to the ship's hold only, especially, if it is not clear whether discharge should be paid by the seller or not.

If the seller does not want to pay any costs after the vessel has arrived to the port of discharge and made herself ready for unloading, he may use the variant "undischarged" to express same explicitly, e.g. "CIF Drammen Incoterms 1990 undischarged". In such case, the buyer pays all costs of unloading the goods from the vessel.

It should be noted that the variant "undischarged" cannot be used in case of liner shipment, or in the case that the buyer could expect the seller to make the contract of carriage on a liner vessel.

The term "free out" is sometimes used to describe the same situation. It is suggested that this ambiguous expression should be reserved for its original purpose, the chartering of ships. "Undischarged" is a term without the burden of any other use.

CFR/CIF landed

On the other hand, parties may decide that the seller pays for the unloading of goods, or to include unloading costs in the sea freight. The parties may also just want to make it clear who would pay the discharge.

The variant "landed" means that the seller has included the costs of unloading in the sea freight which he has paid, or paid them otherwise, e.g. "CIF Grangemouth Incoterms 1990 landed".

CIP loaded

According to CIP, the seller contracts for the carriage to the named destination. That destination may be a terminal, from which the buyer collects the goods. Apart from the freight, the seller also pays for the terminal operations. The costs may be included in the freight or the seller may pay them separately. Terminal costs are often debited in one charge, including discharge into the terminal, handling in the terminal and loading onto the departing vehicle. In such a case it may be in the interests of the seller to extend the seller's costs to cover all terminal operations, that is until the goods are loaded onto the departing vehicle. In such a case, the word "loaded" should be added to the term, e.g. "CIP Duisburg Incoterms 1990 loaded".

DDU cleared

According to DDU, the buyer is responsible for import formalities.

The seller may, however, want to clear the goods for import. In such case, the word "cleared" can be added to the term e.g. "DDU Antwerp Incoterms 1990 cleared". In this case the addition does not affect buyer's obligation to pay the duties (note the letters DU!) neither does it affect seller's obligation to deliver the goods or buyer's obligation to take delivery of them. "DDU cleared" is useful for express freight, where the time of arrival is guaranteed.

DDP VAT unpaid

In DDP, the seller has to bear the risks and costs, including duties, taxes and other charges of delivering the goods, cleared for importation. DDP thus represents the maximum obligation for the seller. Customs administration, however, do not normally grant customs benefits to a foreign company. Therefore, where the seller is unable directly or indirectly to obtain the import licence, DDP should not be used. If it is the buyer who shall clear the goods for importation and to pay the duty, the term DDU should be used instead of DDP.

Where the only element in the clearance is the tax, an addition "VAT unpaid" is available. It indicates that the buyer pays only the tax while the seller clears the goods, e.g "DDP Roissy Incoterms 1990 VAT unpaid". Such variant does not affect the seller's obligation to deliver the goods or the buyer's obligation to take delivery of them.

Conclusion – How to write the variants

Incoterms 1990 give a clear definition for the term of delivery but not for the variants. Therefore variants should not be considered as a part of the term of delivery itself. For the sake of clarity, it is suggested that the variants – the ones described here or other variants mutually agreed between the trading partners – should be written after the reference to Incoterms, e.g. "FCA Bilbao Incoterms 1990 loaded". In this way the term itself and the possible variant are separated from each other and confusions can be avoided

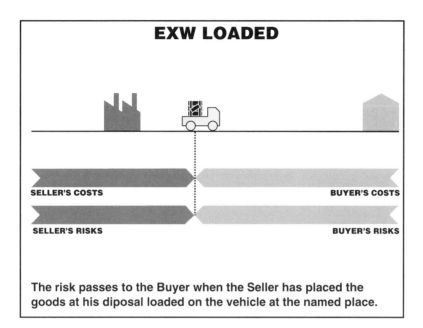

EXW LOADED

SELLER'S COSTS — BUYER'S COSTS

SELLER'S RISKS — BUYER'S RISKS

The risk passes to the Buyer when the Seller has placed the goods at his diposal loaded on the vehicle at the named place.

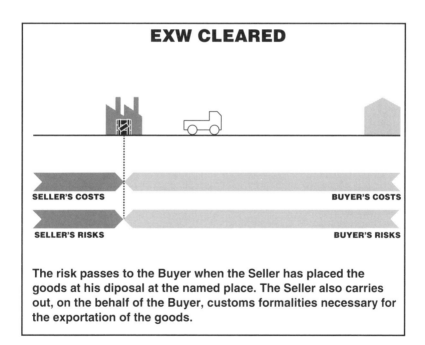

EXW CLEARED

SELLER'S COSTS — BUYER'S COSTS

SELLER'S RISKS — BUYER'S RISKS

The risk passes to the Buyer when the Seller has placed the goods at his diposal at the named place. The Seller also carries out, on the behalf of the Buyer, customs formalities necessary for the exportation of the goods.

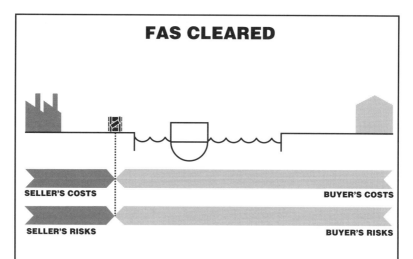

FAS CLEARED

SELLER'S COSTS **BUYER'S COSTS**

SELLER'S RISKS **BUYER'S RISKS**

The risk passes to the Buyer when the Seller has placed the goods alongside the named vessel. The Seller also carries out, on the behalf of the Buyer, customs formalities necessary for the exportation of the goods.

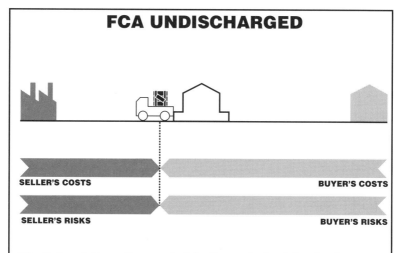

FCA UNDISCHARGED

SELLER'S COSTS **BUYER'S COSTS**

SELLER'S RISKS **BUYER'S RISKS**

The Seller delivers the goods into the custody of the Carrier named by the Buyer by delivering the goods to the terminal to be discharged from the arriving vehicle.

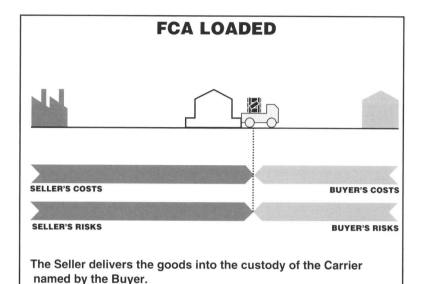

FCA LOADED

SELLER'S COSTS

BUYER'S COSTS

SELLER'S RISKS

BUYER'S RISKS

The Seller delivers the goods into the custody of the Carrier named by the Buyer.

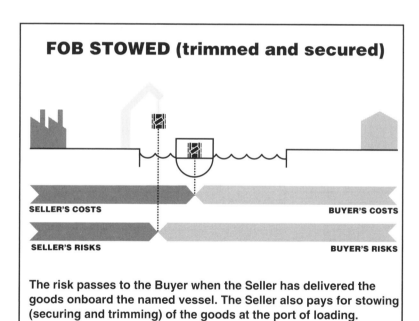

FOB STOWED (trimmed and secured)

SELLER'S COSTS

BUYER'S COSTS

SELLER'S RISKS

BUYER'S RISKS

The risk passes to the Buyer when the Seller has delivered the goods onboard the named vessel. The Seller also pays for stowing (securing and trimming) of the goods at the port of loading.

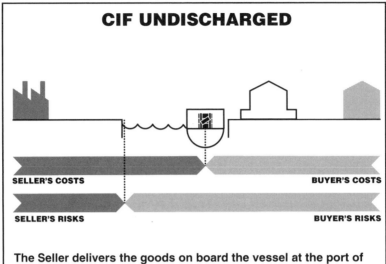

CIF UNDISCHARGED

SELLER'S COSTS

BUYER'S COSTS

SELLER'S RISKS

BUYER'S RISKS

The Seller delivers the goods on board the vessel at the port of shipment and contracts at his expense for the carriage of the goods to the port of destination. The Buyer pays all the costs of unloading from the vessel

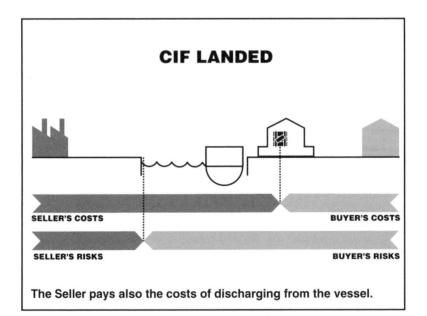

CIF LANDED

SELLER'S COSTS

BUYER'S COSTS

SELLER'S RISKS

BUYER'S RISKS

The Seller pays also the costs of discharging from the vessel.

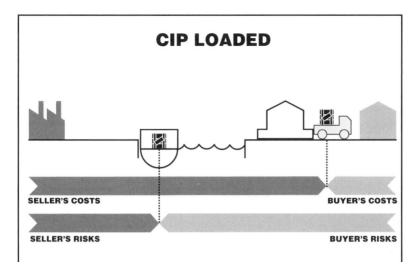

CIP LOADED

SELLER'S COSTS   **BUYER'S COSTS**

SELLER'S RISKS   **BUYER'S RISKS**

The Seller delivers the goods into the custody of the Carrier and contracts for carriage, including the departing vehicle at the place of destination.

Queries on Incoterms

ALEXANDER VON ZIEGLER

General Observation

Four years have elapsed since Incoterms came into force in their new version of 1990. Soon after their publication and distribution throughout the world, the Working Party on Trade Terms realized that Incoterms 1990, as many of the earlier versions have already done before, raise frequent questions of interpretation. While the drafters of Incoterms find many provisions quite clear, the practitioners out in the harbours and business places naturally face some problems in applying Incoterms in their new format. However, it should be noted that the 1990 version of Incoterms brought greater clarity, due to its new layout and systematic compilation. Still, some need for interpretation always remains, even with the most thorough legislation. Therefore, it is not surprising that ICC and other ICC institutions, have recently received numerous questions regarding the new Incoterms. It was then a logical step to create an "Incoterms Panel" within the Working Party on Trade Terms, in order to provide an answering-service for these questions.

In receiving the questions, the Panel noted that most of them did not raise problems related to the nature of Incoterms. Rather, most questions and problems were based on a misunderstanding of the scope and function of Incoterms. The problems were very often outside the scope of Incoterms. They could only be answered by the applicable international or national laws, or by the practice and the customs of the place in question. Therefore, they would not be touched by the Incoterms-framework. For obvious reasons ICC and the Incoterms Panel could not comment on those queries.

The remaining questions, however, went to the very roots of Incoterms. This chapter undertakes to point out the main areas in which those questions arose. Those issues might be looked at as symptoms of a need for further clarification. It will not surprise the reader to find some of the issues raised by the questions covered by special chapters of this book, as for example regarding the Incoterms variants and the Terminal Handling Charges. For obvious reasons it is not possible to identify the individual queries; therefore, this chapter tries to consolidate the issues in a systematic order and will not address each and every query individually.

We will proceed by starting at one extreme, that is at the delivery of the goods at the seller's "works" or premises (governed by the EXW-clause) and travel along the journey until we reach the destination covered by the so-called "D" – Terms (DES / DEQ DDU / DDP).

Ex works – EXW

It is interesting to see that no questions concerned the EXW clause. This is not because EXW is such an easy term. The reason there were no questions relating to EXW might lie in the fact that this clause has remained basically unchanged and therefore no new problems seemed to arise.

Nevertheless, it has to be noted that EXW is far from being an easy clause and that there are many issues which could be raised about this clause.

"F"–Terms

Moving to the "F"- terms we meet the FCA, FAS and FOB terms.

1 Free Carrier – FCA
First of all we shall look at the new FCA clause which was drafted to cover many modes of transportation.

1.1 Terminal Handling Charges
From the first moments of life of this new FCA clause it was clear that the allocation and apportionment of the terminal handling charges would cause considerable controversy. Many shippers and consignees, as well as freight forwarders, encountered difficulties in drawing the line· between the THC elements to be borne by the seller and those to be borne by the buyer. Because of its importance, this subject is covered in Chapter 7 of this book.

1.2 "Handing over"

As regular users of Incoterms will know, the key to the cost and risk allocation is – in the great majority of all incoterms – "delivery" as defined in articles A4 and B4.

In article A4 of the FCA clause delivery is perfected at the time when the delivery of the goods into the custody of the named carrier has been completed. Questions therefore arose regarding exactly when the goods were deemed to have been "handed over" to the carrier. The Panel made clear that the criterion is the **physical transfer of the goods to the carrier** or to its agent. Where people are working with different hats, as for instance freight forwarders, a very careful analysis of the function of those persons is required at the time in question.

1.3 Unloading of truck at export terminal

Related to the problem of the time of the "handing over" is the allocation of the costs for the unloading of the road truck by which delivery to the export terminal is made.

The key again is the criterion of "handing over to the carrier". If it is the road truck personnel who have to unload and hand over the goods to the carrier at the particular place then it will be the responsibility of the seller to bear those costs should they not already be covered by the freight for the inland leg. It is clear from the aforesaid, that the solution will depend upon the particular factual situation, the customs of the port or the usages at the specific terminal concerned.

However, in most cases, the carrier operating the export terminal owns the unloading equipment. It therefore makes sense that the carrier should carry out the unloading and include the costs in the freight to be borne by the buyer.

1.4 Charges in Airport Terminals

The same way aviation law is considered to be the daughter of maritime law, the maritime problem of Terminal Handling Charges has found a little offspring in the form of the problem regarding division of risks and costs in Airport Terminals.

I personally have been flooded by inquiries of freight forwarders or shippers regarding the allocation of specific costs arising after the goods have been delivered to the Airport Terminal for further handling by freight forwarders and handling agents, custom clearance and ultimate loading on the aircraft.

The problem finds its roots in the fact that often the terminal operator also represents the air-carrier (as IATA agent also issuing the air waybill). Therefore handing over to the terminal automatically means handing over to the named carrier and thus will constitute the point of shifting costs and risk to the buyer. This situation is further complicated by the fact that the freight forwarder will organize the custom clearance or otherwise still act on behalf of the shipper/seller, making the seller responsible for those parts of the costs.

This apparent complication can be solved by strictly following the provisions of article A6 for the term FCA, which clearly makes the distinction between the costs relating to the goods including their shipment and handling and the costs relating to the exportation, such as for "customs formalities as well as all duties, taxes and other charges payable upon exportation" (FCA article A6(2)).

2 Free Alongside Ship – FAS

2.1 Transfer of risk

It is interesting to see that some of the queries do not in fact concern Incoterms in the new version of 1990 but could have been asked 20, 30 or even 50 years ago.

Such a query was recently received by the Panel concerning the FAS clause. It concerned a FAS shipment where the seller agreed to deliver "week 33". On Tuesday of that week the seller delivered the cargo to the quay where the vessel was announced to arrive and to load on Thursday of the same week. Before the ship arrived a fire broke out and the goods were destroyed.

Had the risk already passed to the buyer?

The answer to this appears to be quite simple on a reading of article A4: delivery "alongside ship" *requires that there is a ship.* Otherwise we would have to speak of Ex Quay or something along those lines. Delivery under FAS is only perfected if and when the goods are in fact alongside the *ship* waiting to be loaded on board.

The situation as well as the conclusion would be different should the vessel not arrive at the requested time or should the buyer be responsible for irregularities relating to the export licence (FAS, article B2) or fail to give sufficient notice of the arrival of the vessel (FAS, article B7). Here, delivery and, therefore, the transfer of the risk have been perfected as soon as the goods have been duly appropriated to the contract, that is to say, clearly set aside or otherwise identified as the contract goods (FAS, article B5).

3   Free on Board – FOB

3.1   Terminal Handling Charges

Reference is made to Chapter 7 of this book on Terminal Handling Charges.

3.2   Division of costs (THC in transhipment Ports/ loading costs/packaging)

FOB must, together with the CFR/CIF clause, be the most widely used term under Incoterms. For almost a century the term was the subject of numerous court decisions and arbitration awards. This might explain why out of the 27 queries only one was clearly related to this FOB term.

The question was related to the division of costs between the seller and the buyer. More particularly, it concerned costs of terminal handling charges in a subsequent port of transhipment as well as loading and packaging costs.

3.2.1   THC in transhipment Port

Under the FOB term delivery to the ship *in the named* port will shift the costs to the buyer. Whatever costs arise after that moment, it will be the buyer's obligation to pay.

Since Incoterms are nothing but contractual terms, they can, of course, be overridden by contrary language or content of the contract.

3.2.2   Loading Costs

The seller under a FOB contract has to load the goods on board (FOB, article A4). The costs are borne by the seller until the time the goods pass the ship's rail (FOB, article A6). Therefore, under Incoterms it is the seller's obligation to bear in principle the costs of the loading process, unless they are borne by the ship and included in the freight.

Confusion seems to exist between this situation under Incoterms and the division of loading costs under the "Liner Terms". Those "Liner Terms" are not found in the contract of sale but in the contract of carriage between the carrier and the shipper. Apparently, Liner Terms generally include the loading costs in the freight. Since the freight is to be borne by the buyer under incoterm FOB the buyer might as a matter of fact end up also paying for the loading. So far as concerns Incoterms, and more particular the term FOB, however, loading costs are part of loading and therefore, strictly speaking, have to be paid by the seller.

This is a good example of two sets of rules overlapping on, what it seems, similar issues, but on legally totally different layers, one being the contract of sale (Incoterms), the other the contract of carriage of goods by sea (Liner Terms). Since the Liner Terms are not an ICC product the Panel could not give any interpretation regarding those rules.

3.2.3 Packaging

Under Incoterms the costs for packaging the goods are clearly upon the seller (FOB, article A9). Again, on the other layer, i.e. the contract of carriage, it may be that packaging is included in the loading costs and therefore included in the freight collected with the buyer.

From this situation one has to realize that this does not correspond with the contract of sale, since there, under the term FOB, article A9(2), the seller has to provide for packaging "... *which* **is required** *for the transport of the goods, to the extent that the circumstances relating to the transport* (e.g. ***modalities, destination***) *are made known to the* **seller** *before the contract of sale is concluded.*

"C"-Terms

1 General Remarks

Despite the fact that the CFR (commonly know as "C&F") and the CIF terms are the oldest and certainly the most widely used trade terms the "C"-terms remain the most complicated clauses. This is due to the fact that contrary to the "E"-, "F"- and "D"-terms, where only one point in the transport-chain is relevant for delivery as well as for the transfer of costs and risks, the "C"- clauses work with *two* such points:

First, in the *port of loading* delivery takes place, transferring at the same time (more particularly when the goods pass the ship's rail) the risk and parts of the costs.

The second point of relevance is the *port of destination*. It is there where the transport owed by the seller comes to its completion. The freight and all other costs of transportation are to be borne by the seller.

While the rules applicable to the first point, i.e. port of shipment/ loading, follow basically the principles established under the corresponding "F"-Clauses, special problems arise concerning the second point, i.e. the port of destination/discharge.

2 Specific Problems arising under the C-Terms

2.1 Costs at the destination
2.1.1 Costs for unloading the cargo

Regarding this point of destination, problems seem, in particular, to arise in allocating the costs of unloading the goods from the vessel. Are they to be borne by the seller or by the buyer?

First of all let us take into consideration that Incoterms do clearly put the burden for such unloading costs upon the buyer (CFR, article B6) *unless such costs and charges have been levied by regular shipping lines when contracting for carriage...*

Therefore, following the letter of Incoterms 1990, all costs regarding the goods at the port of destination will as a general rule have to be borne by the buyer. It is only where the seller has already contracted for such services and paid the costs as a part of the freight, or otherwise levied by regular shipping lines when the seller contracted for carriage, that the buyer may be relieved from bearing such costs.

2.1.2 Costs "Free out" / "Liner out"

Reading this language one might instantly think of the "Liner Terms" usually providing such an inclusion of the unloading costs into the freight. Many queries have addressed this point. They suggest that CFR or CIF under Incoterms mean to be "free out" or "liner out". As we have seen the cost-allocation in the port of destination will very much depend on the terms for the carriage entered into by the seller and its carrier. It is there where we might indeed find a reference to "Liner Terms" or to "free out" / "Liner out".

It has to be stressed that (first) all these references only concern the contract of carriage, that (second) they are therefore not governed by Incoterms and that (third) the exact meaning of them is vague and ambiguous (see also Guide to Incoterms, page 79).

It is, therefore, recommended that the parties of the <u>contract of sale</u> cover the issue of the costs at the port of destination and clearly define what type of transportation is owed by the seller.

If there is no such specification in the contract, Incoterms put the burden of such unloading costs upon the buyer (CFR, article B6), unless *".... such costs and charges have been levied by regular shipping lines when contracting for carriage...".* An exact allocation of the costs will therefore only be possible after the contractual situation between the seller and the carrier is established. This exact determination of the costs will usually only be possible at a time when the transaction has already been perfected and in some cases even only after the costs have been incurred.

2.1.3 Costs for import clearance

From one query it appeared that in some countries importers buying on CIF terms refuse to pay the costs invoiced to them by the carrier's customs agent for their intervention in the presentation of the customs declaration, verification and control of the merchandise, supervision of the transfer or unloading of the merchandise, etc. Such importers take the position that said costs are included in the transportation price (freight).

However, under the "C"-terms, Incoterms clearly place the costs of import and custom clearance on the buyer (CFR article B6(3)). Therefore, the importers have to pay for costs relating to those formalities, even if invoiced by a carrier's agent.

2.1.4 Quay dues in oil transport

Particular trades require particular applications. This is clearly true for oil transportation, since the cargo in question has particular characteristics and specifications and since special usages prevail in this sector of trade.

In this context queries were addressing the question relating to who had to pay the tax for the use of the oil docks at the port of destination. Since this tax is levied not on the cargo but on the ship it remains a cost for the transportation and will therefore have to be borne by the *seller*. It is clear that this basic rule might be changed by different contractual language or customs of the port that differ from Incoterms. In any case, it is advisable clearly to state in the contract of sale what dues and taxes shall be borne by the buyer, should the parties wish to clarify the situation.

It is of interest that this question was discussed in depth among the members of the Incoterms Panel and of the Working Party on Trade Terms and that it took several meetings to come to a unanimous opinion. However, the result just summarized reflects in my view exactly what the Incoterms say in CIF article A6 : "[The seller must] pay all costs relating to the goods until they have been delivered [...] as well as the freight and all other costs resulting from A3(a)". Such quay dues are exactly such *"costs resulting from CIF article A3 section(a)"!*

2.1.5 CIF "landed"

In an attempt to bring more clarification regarding costs at the port of destination, some parties have started few years ago to insert next to CIF the word "landed", to read "CIF landed port of destination". Some queries have asked the Incoterms Panel to comment on what this variant would mean.

Here I have to stress with all emphasis that this variant, as any other variant, does not belong to the Incoterms family and therefore no interpretation can be given by the ICC. Variants are nothing more than contractual language trying to add something which was not covered at all or not covered sufficiently by Incoterms. Therefore, the solution can only be found in the interpretation of the intentions of the parties, an undertaking which is obviously very difficult when the parties use what they think are customary standard variants of Incoterms.

It is therefore my special advice, particularly from the perspective of my professional position as an attorney, to request that the parties clearly specify what they mean and use extensive wording rather than just referring to variants which have no clear status of interpretation as the Incoterms have.

3 Transfer of risk

The panel further received the following interesting question: Why is the point of transfer of risk the same under CFR and CIF?

The answer is obvious: the only intended distinction between CFR and CIF is that with CIF the costs and obligations of procuring a (minimal) insurance policy are within the responsibility of the seller and are therefore included in the contractual price of the goods. However, the point of transfer of risk is indeed supposed to be the same for the terms CFR and CIF.

In fact one can go further and say that the point for the transfer of risk is also the same as the one applying for FOB contracts!

It is interesting to see that the special nature of the "C"-terms explains why only the "C"-terms address the issue of insurance at all. As we have seen, the "C"-terms work with two points, the port of shipment and the port of destination. Using the "C"-terms it is the seller who chooses the carrier for the transportation to the port of destination. The buyer might have an interest in insuring the goods since he is bearing the risk from the time of the goods passing the ship's rail. In particular, he has, up to the time he takes over the goods at the port of destination, no possibility of intervening with the transportation nor influencing the care and handling of the goods.

4 Insured value 110%

Regarding the insurance cover, it had been questioned why the minimum insurance cover is specified to be the contract price plus 10%. The inclusion of an additional 10% for the insurance cover goes back to the 1906 Marine Insurance Act. The insurance should, in a first layer, in fact cover the value of the goods at the destination which is normally reflected by the CIF/CRF price. This is usually the value at the port of shipment plus the freight and further transportation costs. The insured value should, however, always include a certain average profit which the buyer expects from the use or sale of the goods. Therefore, the drafters of Incoterms 1990 have chosen the customary figure of 110%. This leaves the parties absolutely free to change this in their contract of sale, as they can do for any other term regarding insurance coverage.

5 "Cost & Insurance"

Two queries addressed the issue of the term "Cost and Insurance" or in the short form "C+I".

Here it has to be stressed that Incoterms do not know a term "C+I" and that this term is very ambiguous since its meaning is not clear.

Should the parties mean that the obligation to pay for costs will be terminated in the port of shipment but that the seller should arrange for insurance, then it is most unfortunate to make reference to "C+I", since the "C" suggests that carriage is organized and paid for by the seller. Now, whatever the parties intend the "C+I"-clause to mean it is preferable to either use an "F"-clause, i.e. FCA or FOB named place or port of departure, and in addition define the seller's obligation to provide for an insurance cover. If the parties choose to do so, they are well advised when they clearly specify what type of insurance and what insurance period they mean.

The seller agreed to also bear the costs of transportation and to organize the carriage of the goods recommend to go directly for the well known and established incoterms CIF or CIP as the case may be.

6 "Reasonable time"

Under the 1980 version of Incoterms the seller under a CIF contract was obliged to deliver the goods on board the vessel at the point of shipment "at the date or within the period fixed or, if neither date nor time has been stipulated *within a reasonable time* ...".

If you read the new version of the 1990 Incoterms this provision has been altered to say that the seller must deliver the goods on board the vessel at the port of shipment "at the date or *within the period stipulated*".

One query therefore wondered whether a change was made intentionally by the drafters of the 1990 version. The Incoterms Panel made clear that no change of substance was intended by deleting a reference to the "reasonable time", since such a reference does not add anything to what would apply anyway. If the parties deem the departure time to be essential, they have to stipulate it, whether in the 1980 or 1990 version. Should the parties fail to stipulate either a date or period, then under the 1980 Vienna Convention on the International Sale of Goods, the seller has to do so within a reasonable time. Thus, as a matter of fact, no changes are resulting from the new wording of the Incoterms 1990.

As you can detect from the "C"-terms of Incoterms no reference to the arrival date has been made in them since the crucial delivery moment pursuant to article A4 takes place in the port of shipment and not in the port of discharge. Should the parties and, especially the buyer, request a specific arrival time at the port of destination they would need to stipulate this in their contract of sale. Such a clause may, however, lead to other difficulties. Where the parties agree on a date of arrival, does this mean that the seller bears the risks of late delivery – or, indeed, even of transit loss? Different jurisdictions may give different answers to this question and parties should ask themselves whether they truly want or need to agree on a date for the arrival, as opposed simply to the shipment, of the goods.

"D" TERMS

1 General Remarks

Let us now undertake the last leg of our journey through the transportation-chain and arrive at the so-called "D"-terms which constitute the other extreme of the Incoterms-panorama. Under the "D"-terms the seller undertakes to deliver the goods at a particular point, after the main transportation has already been completed.

As a seller you can sell delivered at the frontier (DAF), ex ship (DES), ex quay (DEQ) or delivered duty either paid or unpaid (DDP/DDU) at a named point.

The Incoterms Panel has received queries only concerning DES and DDU.

Let us quickly look at them. As we do so, it will become clear that many of the problems raised by the queries are very similar to the ones we have detected when discussing the other side of the transportation chain.

2 Delivered Ex Ship – DES

2.1 "No obligation"

Let us first look at one query which represents a great number of inquiries, namely regarding the misunderstanding to what "no obligations" means in Incoterms.

For instance, with respect to the DES incoterm (DES article A3(b)), you will find under "contract of insurance" (on seller's part) the words "no obligation".

This does not mean in any way that the seller bearing the risk until he delivers the goods at the foreign point of destination will have no interest in insuring the goods during the period of his responsibilities. However, the seller does not owe the buyer an obligation to insure the goods. As it is clearly explained in the Guide to Incoterms, Incoterms only specify those obligations owed by one party to the other party. Incoterms do not specify those actions which may be prudent or practical for a party to carry out in its own interest. Therefore, in the case of DES, it may very well be prudent for the seller to take out such insurance, but he has no obligation towards the buyer to do so.

What has just been said also applies for the FOB situation. There, under article A3(a), the seller also has "no obligations" regarding the contract of carriage. Obviously, it is clear that in order to be able to deliver the goods on board the vessel the seller will have to move the goods somehow from his premises and therefore have to organise a sort of contract of transportation/carriage. What is meant by "no obligation", is merely that the seller has to organise everything until he is able to load the goods and that this obligation obviously includes an obligation of the seller to have the goods moved to the port of shipment.

2.2 Quay dues

One other problem relating to the term DES of Incoterms was again the problem of the quay dues. The reader might remember that we have discussed this item when looking at the costs arising in oil trade for the docking of the vessel at the terminal. Again, it was asked whether it was the seller or the buyer who must pay for quay dues (taxes d'accostage) levied upon the ship.

While the delivery is ex ship the ship has to be berthed and therefore the costs the ship has to pay to berth have to be borne by the seller. This is in fact very much in line with what we had said earlier when looking at the CIP situation. In the answer of the Incoterms Panel it was pointed out that when deciding on issues of quay dues one has to carefully look also at the usages/customs of the port or trade or prior course of dealing between the parties, since those could override the principles set out in the Incoterms.

3 Delivered Duty Unpaid – DDU

3.1 Discharge

Under DDU delivery takes place when the goods are placed at the disposal of the buyer in accordance with article A3, that means according to the arrangements of the contract of carriage (DDU articles A4/A3).

In one query the question arose whether, under DDU, it was the seller or the buyer who was responsible for discharging the goods at the named place of destination.

Now, given the definition of delivery under this term, it will be appreciated that Incoterms have not given a clear cut answer regarding the costs relating to the discharge of the goods. In other words, delivery could take place for instance on a truck, as long as the goods are deemed to be at the disposal of the buyer. In such a case, it would be the buyer's obligation to discharge the goods. Incoterms 1990 leave this issue in the hands of the parties and it is therefore necessary to specify in the contract where exactly the goods will be at the disposal of the buyer. It should be stated if this means still on the transportation vehicle (i.e. truck or waggon) or whether the place the goods have to be delivered means "unloaded". In the absence of such a stipulation, the parties will have to look at the customs of the place of destination or at the terms agreed upon between the seller and the carrier regarding transportation to this named point at destination.

3.2 Customs formalities

One query related to the question of customs formalities. The Panel made clear that there could have been some misunderstanding deriving from a misprint in the first printing of Incoterms 1990, which, incidentally, has been corrected since. Under this first print the impression could have been created that the customs clearance was the *seller's* responsibility which is not the case. DDU article B6(3) makes clear that it is the *buyer* who has to pay all duties, taxes and other official charges as well as the cost of carrying out customs formalities payable upon importation of the goods.

It must be emphasized that import responsibilities may be divided into two concepts:

1. customs clearance, administrative formalities such as obtaining necessary licences etc., and

2. duties/import taxes and other official charges, such as VAT.

Thus, although the seller is not responsible for either clearance and duty under DDU, he may agree in the contract of sale to pay the costs for instance of VAT. This should be made clear in the contract for example by adding *"DDU, VAT paid"*.

3.3 Wharfage fee

Related to those last questions of discharging costs and customs formalities is a query asking who had to pay for wharfage fees and landing charges raised by the port authority at destination under the DDU delivery term. Here, Incoterms are clear since they put all costs, duties and taxes as well as official charges connected to the importation of the goods upon the buyer. However, the landing charges and the wharfage fee can both be considered as charges linked to the carriage. Therefore, they should be paid by the seller.

The landing charge is a part of the carriage and the wharfage fee can hardly be considered to be part of costs connected to importation, even if it is based on a custom value. The criteria on which the cost is based are irrelevant since Incoterms only determine the nature of the costs according to the type of activity covered. Moreover, the fact that the wharfage fee was in a particular case levied by a public authority cannot change the findings.

Incoterms in general

1 Recognition

One query asked why certain custom bodies do not accept Incoterms.

First of all it has to be underlined that Incoterms only bind the parties which have incorporated Incoterms in their contract of sale. It will nevertheless have some third party influence since for example third parties like carriers, freight forwarders, insurers etc. will be interested to hear about the division of costs and obligations between the parties. Among the persons interested are the customs authorities.

Now, whether the customs bodies accept Incoterms or not will depend on their knowledge of the matter. It cannot be denied that, worldwide, certain customs authorities work on their special rules and impose either specific terms or refuse references to Incoterms as the case may be.

ICC has done everything possible to inform the custom bodies worldwide but it cannot take further influence on the local customs procedure. Since Incoterms are only contractual terms and have no legislative nature, as conventions have, the individual governments are not bound to recognize the terms agreed by the parties of the transaction.

Therefore, it is suggested that the parties check on the custom regulation in a particular country and then, as the case may be, choose, for the sake of custom formalities, an incoterm acceptable to this authority. Another solution which is not always possible, is to direct the customs authority to the ICC who could verify and certify the authenticity of Incoterms.

2 Payment terms

Another question was whether Incoterms also include definitions of payment such as COD (cash on delivery) or CAD (cash against documents), etc.

When you read the Introduction to Incoterms 1990 you will see that the payment terms are not governed by Incoterms. Therefore, Incoterms will not define COD or CAD terms. The only reference Incoterms makes to the payment is that article B1 Incoterms 1990 specifies that the buyer must pay the price as provided in the contract of sale. With the words "as provided in the contract of sale" it is made clear that, should the parties define specific payment terms as for instance COD or CAD or use a letter of credit, they have to stipulate this in their contract of sale.

3 Modifications

While looking at the different queries, we have touched on several modifications as for instance "CIF Liner out", "C&F Free out", CIF "Landed" or even creations entirely outside the Incoterms world as the term Cost & Insurance "C+I". It has to be emphasized that whenever the parties choose to use modifications they depart from the Incoterms system and therefore leave the "secure land" of international uniform practice and venture on new territories with all risks imminent to such an adventure. It is clear that it is impossible for ICC to advise on the interpretation of such clauses.

The modifications, sometimes referred to as "variants", are covered in Chapter 9 of this book.

4 European Community

Some queries have ventured into the application of Incoterms in the new environment of the European Community /European Union. Reference is made to Chapter 6 of this book.

THE ICC AT A GLANCE

Founded in 1919, the ICC is a non-governmental organisation of thousands of companies and business associations in more than 130 countries. ICC National Committees throughout the world present ICC views to their government and alert Paris headquarters to national business concerns.

The ICC
- represents the world business community at national and international levels;
- promotes world trade and investment based on free and fair competition;
- harmonises trade practices and formulates terminology and guidelines for importers and exporters;
- provides a growing range of practical services to business.

Through its subsidiary, ICC Publishing S.A., the ICC produces a wide range of publications. It also holds vocational seminars and business conferences in cities throughout the world.

Some ICC Services
The ICC International Court of Arbitration (Paris)
The ICC International Maritime Bureau (London)
The ICC Centre for Maritime Co-operation (London)
The ICC Counterfeiting Intelligence Bureau (London)
The ICC Commercial Crime Bureau (London)
The ICC International Bureau of Chambers of Commerce - IBCC (Paris)
The ICC Institute of International Business Law and Practice (Paris)

ICC Publishing S.A.
ICC Publishing, the publishing subsidiary of the International Chamber of Commerce, produces and sells the works of ICC Commissions and experts. It also offers guides and corporate handbooks on topics ranging from banking practice, international commercial arbitration, and joint ventures in the Eastern countries to advertising, environment and telecommunications. Some one hundred titles (in English and French) - designed for anyone interested in international trade - are now available from ICC Publishing. Certain titles also exist in other languages.

For more detailed information on ICC publications and on the above-listed activities, and to receive the programme of ICC events, please contact ICC Headquarters in Paris or the ICC National Committee in your country.

HOW TO BECOME MEMBER OF THE ICC
There are two possible ways of becoming a member of the International Chamber of Commerce: either through affiliation to an ICC National Committee or Group or through direct membership where a National Committee does not exist. For further information, applicants are invited to contact the relevant National Committee or ICC International Headquarters in Paris.

SELECTED ICC PUBLICATIONS

INCOTERMS

Guide to Incoterms 1990
by Jan Ramberg

A companion to Incoterms 1990 (see N°460), the ICC Guide to Incoterms 1990 indicates why it may be in the interest of buyer and seller to use one or another trade term. Each explanation is illustrated with easy-to-understand graphics which show the respective responsibilities of the parties to a transaction. All Incoterms are commented on, clause by clause, to draw the attention of seller and buyer to their respective responsibilities. This guide is an indispensable supplement for exporters/importers, bankers, insurers and transporters, teachers and their students.

E-F	**150 pages - 21 x 28.5 cm**
ISBN 92-842-1088-7	**N° 461/90**

Incoterms 1990

EF-ED-ES-EI	**215 pages - 13.5 x 24 cm**
ISBN 92-842-0087-3	**N° 460**
(other languages available)	

AVAILABLE 1995
Key Words in International Trade (4th edition)

Revised and expanded edition of the ICC's best-selling Key Words containing business words and expressions, translated into English, German, Spanish, French and Italian. Many of the terms are taken from the rapidly changing fields of computing, data processing and telecommunications. Separate alphabetical indexes are included for all languages.

EFDSI   **N° 417/4**

DOCUMENTARY CREDITS

Case Studies on Documentary Credits under UCP 500
by Charles del Busto

This is the first book to analyse in detail real-life cases involving UCP 500. Taken from queries answered by the ICC's Group of Experts, or structured from other cases submitted to the ICC, Case Studies links the UCP Articles with factual explanations concerning their implementation. Each of the 33 case studies in this book is referenced to a specific Article of UCP 500. Each case study is then presented in four parts: Background, Circumstances, Queries and Answers to the Questions. In order to encourage individual training, the answers to the queries are grouped, case by case, in part two. Case Studies is a concrete and practical workbook that you will refer to time and again.

E
ISBN 92-842-1183.2   **N° 535**

Documentary Credits–UCP 500 and 400 Compared
Edited by Charles del Busto

This publication was developed as a highly effective vehicle with which to train managers, supervisors and international trade practitioners in critical areas of the new UCP 500 Rules. A vital companion guide for all concerned with Documentary Credits, it pays particular attention to those Articles that have been the source of litigation.

E	**148 pages - 21 x 29.7 cm**
ISBN 92-842-1157-3	**N° 511**

HOW TO OBTAIN ICC PUBLICATIONS
ICC Publications are available from ICC National Committees or Councils which exist in some 60 countries or from:

ICC PUBLISHING S.A.
38, Cours Albert 1er
75008 Paris (France)
Customer Service:
(1) 49 53 29 23 or (1) 49 53 29 56
Fax: (1) 49 53 29 02 - Telex: 650 770

ICC PUBLISHING, INC.
156 Fifth Avenue, Suite 308
New York, N.Y. 10010
USA
 (212) 206 1150
Telefax (212) 633 6025